Ancient, Medieval and Modern
RHODES

Betty Kayia

ancient, medieval and modern
Rhodes
Ialissos, Kamiros, Lindos

Grecocard Editions
Athens 1996

Editor: George Monemvassitis
General Text Supervision: Betty Kayia
Translation: Marian Grozou
Photography: A. Rodopoulos, L. Hapsis, P. Voukouris, Kostas Tholenos, Stamatis Sofos
Colour Separation: Fotokitaro Ltd.
Maps and Plans: SI Advertising
Plans: Betty Kayia
Printing and Binding: Lithographiko Kentro Ltd.
ISBN: 960-7436-29-6

Dear readers,

As you will discover on reading this book, I have attempted to compile under one cover written records of history and folklore in combination with data gleaned from oral tradition. I have also attempted, without sacrificing scientific accuracy on basic historical and social points, to create pleasant but informative reading matter for islanders and visitors alike. During my few days' stay on the island, I tried to collect as much information as possible. I finished my research in Athens, always with the help of friends from Rhodes who have stood by me all this time. I hope that readers will view my efforts favourably. I would also like to stress that in spite of my honest endeavours and my love for the island, unintentional errors or omissions may have occurred: with your help they can be avoided in future editions.

I feel obliged to inform you that this book would never have come about without the help of the islanders, eponymous and anonymous, who by contributing invaluable information have filled these pages with their knowledge and love of the island. In particular, I would like to thank Kiriakos Finas, mayor of Lindos and distinguished author, who was kind enough to read the whole text. From **Rhodes Town**, Mihalis Balanos, Assistant Mayor of Rhodes; Alexis Papas and Giorgos Mirialakis, merchants; Andreas Sioulas, Director of the Hydrobiological Station; Giorgos Tiliakos, Director of the Municipal Picture Gallery; Angeliki Genikouri, archaeologist; Popi Mahrama, President of tourist/family accommodations; Parthena Kourtidou, employee of the Municipal Library, Giorgos Nikolitsis, city employee; Thanassis Napolitanos, prefectural advisor; Katholiki Kastrouni, Director of the Municipal Cultural Organisation. From **Siana**, Savas Leftopinas, Commune President. From **Arnitha**, Ioannis Tooglou, Commune President, and Giorgos Kostas and Nikos Stergiadis. From **Kritinia**, Maria Hatzinikoli, Commune Secretary. From **Salakos**, Stergos Kipreos, Commune President. From **Ialissos**, Giorgos Hatzikalimeris, Director of the Municipal Cultural Organisation. From **Kremasti**, Stergos Koukias, President, and Stavroula Koukia, Secretary of the Commune. From **Afandou**, Theofanis Pelos, Commune Secretary, and Antonios Nikolis and Sotirios Petrakis. From **Dimilia**, Tsambika Thiriaki, Commune Secretary. From **Lahania**, Ioannis Savakis, Commune President. From **Monolithos**, Emmanuel Maherakis, Commune President. From **Apollona**, Vassilis Sentonas, Commune Secretary. From **Paradissi**, Ioannis Papamanolis, Commune Secretary. From **Kalithies**, Vassilis Sotrilis, Deputy, and Anastasia Politi, Secretary of the Commune. From **Psinthos**, Giorgos Plingos, Commune Secretary. From **Theologos**, Konstandina Stilianou, Commune Secretary. From **Massari**, Tsambika Koulohera, Commune Secretary. From **Malona**, Hrissafina Papageorgiou, Commune Secretary. From **Asklipio**, Giorgos Karageorgiou, Commune Secretary, and Ioannis Pethakas. From **Messanagros**, Mihalis Stamatakis, Commune Secretary, and Mihalis Pizimolas. From **Kalavarda**, Sotiria Sklavouri, Commune Secretary. From **Agios Issidoros**, Evangelos Diakoparaskevas, Commune Secretary. From **Lardos**, Ioannis Flangos, Commune President. From **Apolakia**, Manolis Lergos, Commune President. From **Arhangelos**, Stergos Lambrianos, former Commune President. From **Profilia**, Emmanuel Tsina, Commune President. From **Lindos**, Stefanos Ioannidis, former Mayor of Lindos.

I would also like to thank the Rhodes Harbour Master's Office, Katerina Koutroubaki, employee of the National Tourist Organisation, the Local League of Municipalities and Communes of the Dodecanese for the information they have provided to us, and the Fourth Ephorate of Byzantine Antiquities of the Dodecanese and the 22nd Ephorate of Prehistoric and Classical Antiquities of the Dodecanese for allowing us to take photographs.

Betty Kayia

Table of Contents

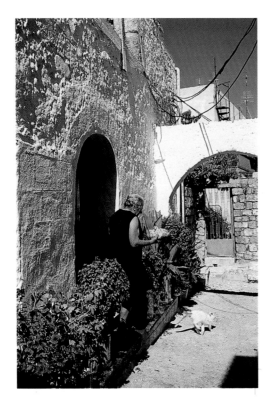

Polybius the Megalopolitan acknowledges the Rhodians' supremacy on the seas, "...because they were looked on as rulers, as masters of the seas."

Strabo relates: "The city of the Rhodians lies on the eastern tip of the island, and differs from other cities in the construction of the harbours, streets, walls and every other structure; thus it can be said that among the other Greek cities none comes close to being its equal, much less its superior." On the Rhodians' strength on the seas, Strabo comments: "This, too, is said of the Rhodians, that even long before the Olympic games began they travelled far from their homes

Rhodes' key geographic position, its excellent climate, strong commercial ties, and the tendency developed by the seafaring Rhodians to found colonies throughout the known world have all played a positive part in its evolution. As a result of those factors, its history was a tumultuous one, and it came to occupy a prominent position among the main agents which caused the Greek spirit to flourish.

Famous from the most ancient of times, Rhodes became a point of reference for men of intellect. Homer extolled the prosperity of the Rhodians, who "...enjoyed the smiles of Zeus the Son of Cronos... who filled their treasuries with untold wealth."

in ships for people's salvation."

To Lucian belongs the famous saying: "Indeed, the city of Helios is worthy of the god in beauty."

On the city's fortifications, Aelius Aristides wrote: "A wonder of which the eyes could not get enough was the circle of walls and their lofty, handsome towers, which looked like torches.
And thus it happened that those arriving in Rhodes by sea saw its walls and its towers, and felt their morale and in their spirit being raised."

The ancient Rhodians themselves said proudly of their powerful navy:

"Out of ten of us Rhodians, ten are sailors."

From literary sources we learn that the Rhodians built their houses, impressive in size and ornamentation, "to last forever".

Dapper mentions that, during its period of development, "Rhodes was a repository of the Arts and Sciences, and at the same time of men of learning."

Cristoforo Buondelmonti toured all the islands of the Aegean, and had the following to say characteristically of Rhodes: "In Rhodes, no matter how much it rains, the sun comes out at least once a day."

7

Introduction

Rhodes is Greece's fourth largest island in area, and the biggest and most famous island of the Dodecanese (area 1,412 square kilometres). It is shaped like a diamond that bulges out in the centre, and its northern tip lies only 15 nautical miles from the coast of Turkey, towards which it is turned. Given its situation far from the world of mainland Greece, and the absence of an important Asian city on the coast opposite, remote Rhodes depended on its naval strength to escape from its geographic isolation and establish ties with the known ancient world, by serving as a link between the Aegean, Crete, Asia Minor, Cyprus and the East.

Rhodes lies at a distance of 250 nautical miles from Piraeus. Surrounding it are the islands of Halki and Alimia, and the rocky islets of Atrakoussa (ancient Tragoussa), Makri, Strongili, Drossonissi, Htenia or Strongilo, Prassonissi (off the island's southern coast), Galouni, and Pentanissos or Tetrapoli.

Rhodes is a mountainous island; its highest peak is that of Mt. Ataviros (1,215 m.), which forms part of a range stretching to include Mt. Akramitis or Gramithi (823 m.) in the northwest. Further to the east stands thickly forested Mt. Profitis Ilias (800 m.).

The island's geographical position has given it all the features of a Mediterranean climate, with mild winters and abundant rainfall, as well as cool – thanks to sea breezes and westerly winds – but sunny summers. This climate has also favoured cultivation of the land: the fertile plains (18 per cent of the island's total area) saw the development of agriculture (cultivation of olive- and other fruit-trees, vegetables, grapes) and stock-breeding (grazing land constitutes 34 per cent of the island's total area; it has supported sheep, goats, horses and cattle since the most ancient of times). Other well-developed areas are

Imposing Mt. Ataviros rises above the village of Embona.

Deer in Rodini Park

apiculture, wine-making, fishing and tobacco-growing. The significant drop in the number of islanders engaged in these activities is due to the development over the past few decades of tourism, which is now the pre-eminent productive sector, on which the island's whole economy is based.

Rhodes has quite a few seasonal torrents, but no river of any note. The largest river is the Gadouras, between Kalathos and Massari. Outstanding among the

You will spend your holidays awash in sun and sea.

many springs, forests (37% of the island's total area) and lush valleys are the Valley of the Butterflies and the Seven Springs. Rhodes' forests are home to a rare species of fallow deer, Dama dama. The City of Rhodes keeps a few in the castle moat (now dry), to preserve the species. Their odour is believed to repel snakes – as prophesied by the Delphic oracle. Hunting them is forbidden, but for lovers of the sport, the island offers quail, woodcock, hare and wild duck hunting at certain times of the year.

Thanks to the rapid growth of tourism, Rhodes is a real paradise for sports aficionados. Ideal for every type of water sport (swimming, snorkeling, water-skiing, wind-surfing, sailing), it also boasts basketball courts, tennis courts and golf courses in most luxury hotel complexes. The choice of dishes served by the countless restaurants, tavernas and fast-food outlets varies as to price and specialty, from traditional food to international cuisine. And Rhodes' piano bars, discos, Greek music halls and cinemas provide a vibrant variety of high-quality entertainment.

The island today comprises 41 villages, three municipalities and two settlements. Its population is 98,146 (1991 census). Its innumerable natural beauty spots, excellent climate, with 262 days of sun out of 365, important historic monuments, superb road network and frequent service by sea, air and road to the island's points of interest, ultra-modern hotel accommodations and associated tourist installations have made Rhodes a cosmopolitan resort of international renown.

What's in a Name

Ancient place-names are always associated with mythological tradition, ethnic and historical consciousness, or even physical characteristics of a specific locale. The name Rhodes has remained unchanged since ancient times; it is believed to have been taken from the bride or daughter of the sun-god Rhodus or from the flower of the Pomegranate ("Rhodon"), thought to be pictured on coins dating from the 4th, 5th and 6th centuries BC. The flower on the coins may, however, be a rose-bud.

A plethora of epithets have also been bestowed on the island, among them "Telchinis" (= charming, island of the Telchines), "Macaria" (= felicitous, or from a son of Macarus, who founded a colony on Rhodes), "Asteria" (= from the sixth daughter of Phoebe and Coeus, first of the Titans), "Helioussa" (= nymph of the sun), "Aethraea" (= windy), "Ophioussa" (= island of snakes), "Ataviria" (from the mountain of the same name).

Mythology

The myths associated with the powerful kingdom of Rhodes are many and varied. Contributing to this variety were the arrivals of different tribal groups, memories of geological phenomena, which had to be justified in some way since the original events had been forgotten, as well as the island's natural charm. Some mythographers relate that Rhodes existed from the time the world came into being, but it was covered by swamps, which the Sun (Helios) dried up, whence its name Helioussa. Others say that it arose out of the waves – a myth with accords with the area's turbulent geological past.

The first tribe of Rhodes for whom we have a name, the Telchines, were sons of Pontus and of the Earth. Some say they were the dogs of Actaeon, in human form, which had devoured their master; or sons of Tartarus – a place as far below the earth as heaven is above the earth – and the goddess of justice Nemesis; or that they sprang up from the blood of Uranus, when he was dismembered by his son, Cronus.

Helios, the sun god, and the "Rhodon" flower are pictured on Rhodes' ancient coins after 408/7 BC.

According to the famous geographer Strabo (64 BC – AD 19), they came from Cyprus via Crete. They were strange demonic beings, surrounded by legends imbued with fear and awe. Of evil soul and repulsive appearance, they lived both on the land and in the water, like amphibians. As their name (from the ancient verb "thelgo" = to charm) implies, they were enchanters, that is, they were regarded as miracle-makers, who could make it rain, hail or snow, throw down lightning-bolts or metamorphose themselves. Spirits of metals, fine sailors and renowned inventors of arts, as the historian Diodorus the Sicilian tells us, they worked gold, bronze and iron [Cronus' harpe (= curved sword from northwestern Asia Minor), Poseidon's trident], and were the first to fashion statues of gods that could walk (like those Daedalus made in Crete), among them Telchinian Apollo, Telchinian Hera, the Nymphs of Camirus, etc.! The Lindian historian, Timachidas, reports in his *Chronicle of the Sanctuary of Lindus* that the Telchines had dedicated to the temple of Lindian Athena a crater made of an unknown material!

Cronus took the place of his father Uranus and married his sister Rhea, in the knowledge that he would be dethroned by one of his children, so he swallowed them as soon as they were born. Rhea, who could not bear to have any more children disappear, gave Cronus a mule to swallow and entrusted her newborn son (Poseidon) to the care of the Telchines and Capheira, daughter of Ocean. Strabo (I.3) adds that

11

Hellenistic marble head of Helios, from the medieval town of Rhodes (Rhodes Archaeological Museum)

nine of the Telchines followed Rhea to Crete, undertook the rearing of Zeus, and were named "Curetes".

Their myth concludes with their diaspora during the flood brought about by Zeus or Apollo because of their evil nature. According to another tradition, they were expelled from the island by the Heliades, who symbolised enlightened civilisation which eschews sorcery and occult practices. As they left, they are said to have made the island barren by watering it with the terrible water of the River Styx – Styx, the daughter of Ocean, was a fearsome deity, despised by the immortals [according to the didactic epic poet Hesiod (ca. 750-700 BC)].

As an adolescent, Poseidon fell in love with the sister of the Telchines, the nymph Alia – sole heiress to the island – and by her had 6 sons and a daughter, the nymph Rhodus. When Aphrodite inspired a revengeful frenzy in Alia's proud, abusive sons, they succumbed to the greatest moral weakness (immorality) and forced their mother to commit unnatural sexual acts with them. Their father exiled them to the centre of the earth, and Alia fell into the sea and was honoured with the name of "Leucothea". Some say that Rhodos was the daughter of Aphrodite, or the daughter of Poseidon and the nereid Amphitrite.

In the 5th century BC, the Theban lyric poet Pindar (513-438 BC) wrote his *seventh Olympian Ode* in honour of the Rhodian victor in the Olympic Games, Diagoras. This epinician hymn is considered to be the most important source for the island's mythical background. When Zeus conquered the Giants and distributed the land among the gods of Mt. Olympus, Helios was absent on his daily journey and was not dealt a lot. The father of the gods realised his mistake and suggested casting lots again, but Helios asked to be given the island of Rhodes, which he had chosen, when he saw it rise slowly out of the depths of the sea. He made Lachesis, the Fate of the future, swear that the island would be a permanent prize for him, and that it would bloom, and it was so. From Pindar, we learn of the ancient Rhodians' strange custom of dedicating a chariot to Helios each year, like the one they believed he used to travel over the world, by pushing it into the sea. When the new city had been established, they instituted the Alieia, a festival in honour of "Alios" (Helios in the Doric dialect). Celebrated every five years, it included a procession, sacrifice and boys' and men's games.

The children of Helios and Rhodos, the seven Heliades, occupied themselves with education, astrology, astronomy and shipping. But once they quarrelled and killed the first Heliad, Tenages. Then they were forced to split up: Macarus went to Lesbos, Candalus to Kos, Actis to Egypt, Triopas to Caria, and the two who had not taken part in the murder (Ochimus and Cercaphus) built Achaea (ancient Ialysus). Ochimus married the nymph Hegetoria and by her had a daughter, Cydippe or Cyrbia, who married her uncle, Cercaphus. When Cercaphus died, his children, Camirus, Ialysus and Lindus, divided their ancestral land into three parts and founded their three namesake cities.

Other settlers on the island included the Phoenicians, a people of sailors and founders of colonies from Phoenicia (present-day Lebanon). Led by Cadmus, son of their king, Agenor, they reached Rhodes. As Cadmus and his mother Telephaessa wandered in search of his sister Europa, who had been abducted by Zeus in the form of a bull, they stopped in Rhodes, where he erected a temple to Poseidon. The god's priests attributed the introduction of his cult to Cadmus, whom Poseidon had saved from a storm at sea. According to Diodorus the Sicilian, the Phoenician alphabet entered Greece via Rhodes, because Cadmus dedicated to Athena a bronze basin bearing a Phoenician inscription. The Phoenicians spread throughout the whole island; their presence was strongest in Camirus.

When the Calydonians fought the Thesprots led by Heracles, and the city of Ephyra fell, Heracles killed its king, Phyleas, and married his daughter Astyocheia, with whom he had a son, Tlepolemus. In the *Iliad* (Book II), Homer relates how, when Heracles died, Tlepolemus came to Argolis, where he accidentally killed his father's uncle, the King of Tiryns, Lycimnius, with a club of olive-wood. In order to escape the wrath of the other sons and grandsons of Heracles, he heeded the advice of the Delphic oracle and went to a land where the Sun and Zeus were worshipped, to found a Dorian colony. Pindar tells us that he went to Rhodes and Zeus gave him riches, which he used to repair and fortify the island's three cities. Also in Book II of the Iliad, Homer informs us that Tlepolemus took part in the Trojan War with nine ships. The poet Lycophron (3rd century BC) provides information about Rhodes' shipping and colonising activities during Tlepolemus' time. He was finally killed in a duel with the King of the Lycians, Sarpedon, son of Zeus and Europa and ally of the Trojans. The Rhodians honoured his memory in the Tlepolemia festival. One myth has it that Tlepolemus named ancient Rhodes' three cities after the three daughters of Danaus, who died on the island.

After Tlepolemus' death, his wife Polyxo ruled Rhodes. According to the geographer and traveller Pausanias (2nd century AD), Helen of Troy took refuge on the island, pursued by the relatives of the unjustly killed warriors, and asked her fellow-countrywoman, Polyxo, to help her. But the queen, who held her responsible for her husband's death, pretended to welcome her, only to have her seized while she was bathing, and hanged from a tree. Later the islanders erected a temple in honour of "Helen of the Tree". According to one legend, tears dripped constantly from the fateful tree, and were believed to be those of the hanged queen. Among the descendants of Tlepolemus, called Eratides (from Eratus, King of Argos, Tlepolemus' birthplace) was the Olympic victor Diagoras.

When the ship of the matricide Orestes got caught in a storm, it put in at Rhodes.

History

Prehistory

When the land that is now Greece began to be formed about 30 million years ago, most of the Aegean islands were connected to each other, except for those

The chariot of the sun god, now in the Vatican Museum

The ancient city of Camirus, built like an amphitheatre

which lay close to the coast of the mainland and formed part of it. At that time, Rhodes was joined to Asia Minor. After the geological upheavals brought about in the Tertiary Period by volcanic eruptions and disintegration of mountains caused by torrential rains, the islands separated. The myth that Rhodes rose out of the sea echoes actual geological phenomena, attested to by the seashells to be found on the island's highest peaks.

Between the 4th and 3rd millennia BC, the people living on the Aegean islands and the coast of Asia Minor developed the first important Greek civilisations (5000-1100 BC). Opinion is divided among archaeologists with regard to the origins of the people inhabiting the island at that time. P. Waltz, professor at the University of Clermont-Ferrand, states that Rhodes, which stood on one of the principal crossroads of the Eastern Mediterranean, was colonised, after Crete, by peoples whose origins were in the steppes of the East. The island's dense population belonged to the Aegean tribe. Its people produced important artefacts, and worked in copper mines. The English archaeologist Sir Arthur Evans (1851-1941) believed that before the island broke off from the mainland, the area was inhabited by Cretans, and that around 3500 BC it received peoples from the NE Libyan region (the Nile Delta) who were being persecuted by the Egyptian kings. The German archaeologist

and architect Wilhelm Dörpfeld (1853-1940) believed that they were Pelasgians and Carians who had first settled in Crete, whereas the Greek archaeologist H. Tsoundas (1857-1934) was of the opinion that they were pre-Hellenic Pelasgians, tribes related to the Carians. Finally, the professor of history P. Karolidis (1849-1934) believed that they came from Crete and Asia Minor, and belonged to the Arian race (white Asian and European race). Today it has definitely been confirmed that the first inhabitants of Rhodes originated in the Helladic area, as did all the island's colonists. A few desultory preliminary investigations of the caves of Koumelos Arhangelos (4000-3400 BC) and Agios Georgios Kalithies (5000-3700 BC) brought to light artefacts from the Neolithic era.

From the Early and Middle Bronze Age, only a few stone objects were found in Lindus and Ialysus. Next to settle on the island were, according to Diodorus the Sicilian, the Telchines of myth (Cretans), who inhabited the island between the end of the Stone Age and the middle of the Bronze Age (2400-1200 BC). According to Strabo, they worked in bronze and iron. Between 1550 and 1450 BC, they settled in Ialysus and created an important Late Mycenean settlement.

The Mycenean finds from all over the island are evidence that Rhodes was first settled throughout almost its whole territory in the same period. Around 1500 BC, according to the written evidence, the Telchines were superseded by the Achaeans (Myceneans). When they appeared, they ousted or subjugated the Cretans of Ialysus (1350 BC). They spread, not always peaceably, to Ialysia, Camirus, and later to almost the whole island. On the northwest side of the island, they fortified a hill (present-day Filerimo), which was known as "Achaea" until the 3rd century BC.

Around the 15th century BC, the three most important Early Hellenic centres of civilisation, Lindus, Camirus and Ialysus, also received Phoenician colonists. Later the Dorians descended from the north and established themselves on the shores of the Aegean prior to their so-called invasion of the rest of Greece. That is why this area, including Caria, was named "Doris". They arrived on Rhodes under their mythical king Tlepolemus, possibly from Argos [Homer dates them before the Trojan War (Mycenean Era), but genealogically he places them 80 years after the Trojan events (1104 BC)]. The death of King Tlepolemus marked the end of the existence of a powerful central leader (inherent in the way the Mycenean state was organised), and the island was divided into three cities.

Historical Epoch

For most of the islands of the Aegean, the years between the 12th and the 10th centuries BC are considered to have been a dark age. Their reverberations in literature go under the name of "Trojan". That appears to have been the period when the three city-states began to take shape politically; due to their common racial origin, they coexisted peacefully, developing their resources to the full.

Rhodes retained the leadership of the Aegean islands for a long period of time. Between the 8th and the 6th centuries BC, Lindus followed the course taken by the Ionian cities in trade, shipping and shipbuilding, and played the leading role in Rhodian colonisation (main colonies at Faselis and Soloi in the East, and at Gela and Acragas in the West). As a result, the island monopolised commercial transactions throughout the Mediterranean and Black Seas. In contrast, Ialysus and Camirus had more of an aristocratic system based on an agricultural economy, because of the fertile land in which they lay. In 660 BC they formed a "kingless oligarchic federation", and their ruler was

Lindos' fortress reaches up in a desperate attempt to touch the sky.

elected from the royal family of Ialysus. Each city kept its internal autonomy and elected a local council, the "mastroi". Legislative power consisted of the council and the executive, made up of five prytanes who were changed every six months. The highest ruler was the priest of the Sun.

For reasons already stated at the beginning of this chapter, the Dorian Hexapolis was founded in 700 BC. It was a religious and political alliance between the Dorians on the Aegean islands and the coast of Asia Minor, centred around the sanctuary of Apollo on Cape Triopio on the Cnidos peninsula. It was made up of Lindus, Camirus, Ialysus, Kos, Cnidos and Alicarnassus (the latter two being cities of Caria in Asia Minor). The ancient historian Thucydides (455-396 BC) informs us that the Hexapolis became a Pentapolis when, after his victory in the games of Triopian Apollo, king Agasicles of Alicarnassus took his trophy (a bronze tripod) home with him instead of dedicating it, as was befitting, to the temple of the god, where the council of the Hexapolis met (Book I, 144).

Rhodes had ties to the whole known world, and, to facilitate commerce, Lindus and Camirus began to mint their own coins in the 6th century BC. Ialysus followed during the next century. The Rhodian monetary system was regarded as a prototype in its time: Rhodian coins were in circulation throughout the known world, and it is even said that at least eight of the pieces of silver for which Judas betrayed Christ were minted on Rhodes!

After the Ionian cities rebelled (499-494 BC), the Persians sailed into the Aegean for the first time in 491 BC, for the purpose of punishing all the cities which had aided the Ionians in their revolution. The leader of the expedition was Darius and Datis was his general. Their first stop was Rhodes, which put up a heroic resistance.

Datis also attacked the Acropolis of Lindus, and kept it under siege for some time. Finally, as Timachidas tells us in the Chronicle of the Sanctuary, *the inhabitants ran out of water and would have had to surrender, were it not for the goddess Athena, who appeared in a dream to the ruler and assured him that her father would not leave the city in the lurch: he would send rain. The besieged asked if they could postpone their surrender for five days, and Datis laughed when he learned what the reason was. The next day clouds began to gather over the city, and the frightened Persians retreated, but not before making lavish dedications at the temple of Athena.*

Ten years after their defeat at Marathon, the Persians tried to invade Greece for a second time. Up to then Rhodes had been under an obligation to give Xerxes 40 warships each year. Xerxes himself led the expedition, and Mardonius was his general. They set out in the spring of 480 BC from Sardis (capital of Lydia in Asia Minor). In the decisive battle of Salamis (in September of 480 BC), Rhodes was forced to send 40 ships to fight on the side of the Persians.

After the Persian Wars, Rhodes' three cities joined the First Athenian Confederacy (478-477 BC), the better to protect themselves against the Persians. The onerous contributions the allies had to make to the common treasury enhanced the Athenians' power and created dissatisfaction among the smaller cities, which developed a desire for independence. The isolated rebellions of Euboea, Samos, Megara and Mytilene showed that Athens was strong enough to overcome any obstacle, in order to keep its place in the alliance. None of this escaped the notice of Dorieus, famed descendant of the Diagoridae and victor in the Olympic Games; he realised that only a strong and united Rhodes would be able to escape from Athenian hegemony.

The year 431 BC marked the beginning of the terrible Peloponnesian War, and in 427 BC Dorieus and his nephew Peisirhodus, taking advantage of the general ill-feeling towards the Athenians, took the side of the Spartans (Diodorus the Sicilian). The rebellion was quelled. Urged on by Dorieus, the Rhodians revolted again in 411 BC, after the Spartans' victory in Syme (where Dorieus had taken part). That same year he called the island's elders together at the sanctuary of Lindian Athena, where it was decided to synoecise, or unite, the three cities under one capital city. During the Hellenistic Era the form of government of the new entity was democratic. The priest of the Sun, who was the eponymous archon, served a term of one year. The council and the five prytanes were replaced every six months, and comprised the state's executive power.

The island served as a base of operations for the Spartans until 404 BC, when the devastating civil war ended in an overwhelming victory for the Spartan Lysander at Aigospotamoi. From 411 to 377 BC, the democratic and oligarchic factions, almost equal in strength, vied for supremacy in the new city. Luckily this did not have an unfavourable impact on the island's flourishing economy. Later Rhodes joined the Second Athenian Confederacy (377 BC), which broke up after the war between the allies.

The oligarchs found their representative in the person of the satrap of Caria, Mausolus (377-353 BC). When he died, he was succeeded by his sister and wife,

Artemisia the Younger, who, with the assistance of the oligarchs, took the fleet, slaughtered the sailors, entered the city and put all dissenters to death. She erected the celebrated Mausoleum (one of the Seven Wonders of the World) for her dead husband, and died of grief two years after his death.

In the middle of the 4th century BC, a new power made its appearance in the Greek world: the Macedonians, whose objective was the national unity of Greece. When their King, Philip II (382-336 BC) died and was succeeded by his son Alexander the Great (356-323 BC), the clear-sighted Rhodians, foreseeing his victories, were careful to secure favourable treatment. They accepted the Macedonian garrison Alexander left behind him on the island, as well as the gifts he offered to the temple of Lindian Athena (Lindian Chronicle). Nevertheless, two great Rhodian generals, the brothers Mentor and Memnor, distinguished themselves in the Persian camp. Modern-day historians claim that if the Persians had not been distrustful of their plans, they might have managed to check Alexander himself.

The announcement of Alexander's death reawakened the resistance of the Greek cities, and Rhodes threw off the Macedonian yoke. In this case the Rhodians attempted, as they were to do repeatedly in the future, to manoeuvre diplomatically, by pursuing a neutral, independent foreign policy. This was a necessary prerequisite for carring on normal trade and shipping, which allowed the Rhodians to stay in first place in the Grecian world. In pursuit of this time-honoured policy, they refused to ally themselves with the Macedonian King Demetrius I "The Besieger" (337-283 BC) or his son Antigonuo Gonatas (318-239 BC) against Ptolemy I of Egypt. So in the summer of 305 BC, Demetrius began the siege of the well-fortified city of Rhodes. Despite the numbers of footsoldiers and cavalry, and the large

Like many other places throughout the town, the main courtyard of the hospital/archaeological museum contains stone cannon- or catapult-balls left over from the many sieges Rhodes has undergone.

fleet of the besiegers (40,000 men, 400 ships and impressive siege artillery), the city put up a heroic resistance (*Pausanias' Guide to Greece*, I. 6).

In repeated attacks, Demetrius, who had not earned his title of "the Besieger" for nothing, set up his floating catapults opposite the city walls. But the Rhodians, led by their admiral, Execestrus, boarded three "kamikaze" ships, and, approaching the ships supporting the catapults, sank them by ramming into their bottoms. When bow-strings got low, the brave women of Rhodes used their long tresses to string the warriors' bows.

Finally, the two sides were forced to cease hostilities, after the intervention of ambassadors from the Aetolian Confederacy! Its successful resistance to this siege increased Rhodes' prestige among the powers of that age.

The severe earthquake of 227/6 BC caused great devastation, judging from Polybius' description of it. But it did not hold back development on Rhodes, because in a collection taken up among all the Greek city-states, many leaders who were hostile to each other competed in offering monetary and other gifts, and granting "immunity" (= exemption of Rhodian ships which put into their ports from customs duties). This shows that Rhodes was a naval power of great importance in distributing their products in foreign markets. Thus the damage from the earthquake was quickly repaired. In 220 BC, Rhodes, with enhanced prestige and reputation, went to war with Byzantium and forced it to abolish the tax which it had imposed on grain imported from the north shore of the Black Sea (referred to as the "paragogium" by Polybius, IV.37, 38, 47-53). But in general Rhodes combated the pirates who infested the seas at that time, and protected commerce.

In the war between the Romans and the Macedonian King Philip V (221-179 BC), Rhodes – in defence of its economic interests – together with the leader of Pergamum Attalus II (220-138 BC), presented the Romans with a fleet so that they could liberate the Cyclades. In 188 BC, according to the Roman historian Titus Livius (59 BC-17 AD), Rome ceded Lycia and Caria to the Rhodians, as a reward for their invaluable alliance against Antiochus III of Syria in the naval battle at Side in Pamphylia in 190 BC.

Today we are in a position to say that these moves proved fatal, since the Macedonians were the last bastion against the Romans. The Carthaginian general, Hannibal, military advisor to Antiochus III, dedicated his book on the works of the Romans in Asia to the Rhodians, to show them what they had to expect from the brief friendship of the Romans!

In 167 BC, after repeated, long-drawn-out conflicts with the Macedonians, the Romans exploited the discord among the Greek cities and occupied Greece, which became a Roman province. They wrested from the Rhodians their possessions in Lycia – upon the request of the Lycians themselves to the Roman Senate – and in Caria, because Rhodes did not want to get involved in the Third Macedonian War between the Romans and the successor of Philip V, Perseus (178-167 BC). A year later, the income of the Rhodian state was reduced even further, and its economy weakened significantly, when the Romans declared the island of Delos a free port. (Rhodes' income from duties on goods in transit fell from a million drachmae to 150,000!) In 164 BC, Rhodes was forced to enter into a treaty on humiliating terms, by which she effectively lost her independence.

Early in the first century BC, the ambitious King of Pontus, Mithridates VI, son of Eupator (132-63 BC) allied himself with Cilician and Cretan pirates and clashed with the Romans, thereby inciting the Greeks to revolt. Rhodes, necessarily an ally of the Romans in all their military enterprises, remained faithful to its alliance and offered asylum to Roman fugitives. For that reason, Mithridates laid siege to it for several months in 88 BC, during which the island once again demonstrated just how well organised its defences were.

After that, Rhodes became an even more devoted camp-follower of the Romans, and suffered the consequences of the civil wars between the Roman emperors. First it took the side of Pompey (Battle of Pharsalia, 48 BC), later of his opponent, Caesar, and after the latter's assassination, of the vindicators of his death. Their opponent, Cassius Parmensis (87-42 BC), beleaguered the city, despite the fact that he had studied there. Indeed, it is said that when his Rhodian teacher, Archelaus, tried to make him change his mind, Cassius scoffed at him, saying "I will leave you your sun!" In 42 BC he conquered Rhodes and stripped it of every item of value, including about 3,000 statues from the temples, which he used for the beautification of Rome, according to the Roman sage Pliny the Elder (AD 23-79)!

When the Emperor Octavian vanquished Antony and Cleopatra in the Battle of Actium (31 BC), he granted Rhodes the title of allied city and used it as a place of exile for politicians. The Roman Emperor Vespasian (AD 70-79) included it in the Roman Empire.

Ancient Rhodes

The site chosen in 411 BC to build the new city of Rhodes was on the island's northeast tip (Panos akran), overlooking the strait that controlled the sea route between the Aegean and the East.

Prehistoric tools and pottery from the Middle Bronze Age found in the eastern harbour indicate that this site, ideal for facilitating transport and commercial traffic, was inhabited well before the new city was founded. The area appears to have remained in continuous habitation until the beginning of the 5th century BC.

A leading role in the procedures to

Figure I: Plan of the ancient city, based on a topographical plan by I. Kondis and K. Doxiadis

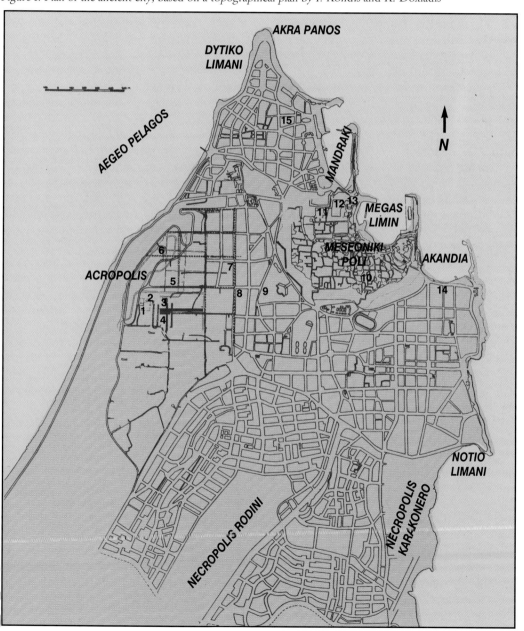

abolish the form of government existing up to that time and to synoecise the three city-states was played by Diagorides Dorieus, using a plan he had devised while he was ostracised in Thurium in Italy. The "Rhodian Damos" was designed, according to Strabo (*Geographica*, IV. 2) by the father of systematic town-planning, the architect Hippodamus the Milesian (who planned the city of Piraeus) or at least in the "Hippodamian manner". Construction was completed on 408/7 BC, and today it is one of the most magnificent examples of an organised Greek city.

Excavations have demonstrated that there was no exaggeration in the praises that ancient authors heaped on the new city's excellent grid plan and general layout.

The fortifications of 408/7 BC consisted of two parallel rows of large blocks of porous stone; the gap between them was filled with small stones, earth and other materials. These walls proved inadequate, according to Diodorus, in the flood of 316 BC, in Demetrius' siege of 305/4 BC, and in the earthquake of 227/6 BC. They were finally replaced, as related by Polybius, by new, more compact walls, adapted to the new requirements of the art of besiegement. These were made of two or three rows of stone blocks, with strong rectangular or semicircular towers and bastions. The new circuit ran the length of the shore and encompassed the acropolis and its sanctuaries. Authors in Roman times attest to the good condition of the walls well into the second century AD. Pausanias states that only Messenia had a better citadel than Rhodes. Later, the Romans destroyed the walls in many places, and they never allowed the Rhodians to repair them.

Also ideal was the lay of the land in the area chosen to build the new city. Its acropolis stood on the hill of Agios Stefanos, the town's westernmost and highest point (elevation: 111 m.). Here the steep declivity down to the sea creates a natural fortification. In a temenos on the top of the hill stood the temple of Zeus Polieus and Athena Polias and a large building with a stoa (Fig. I, 6).

Sanctuaries of secondary importance were the nymphaea (Fig. I, 5), cave-like underground chambers used as places of recreation and worship, perhaps of the Nymphs (semi-divine beings inhabiting forests, bodies of water, etc.). After the excavations carried out in 1924-29, the temple of Pythian Apollo (Fig. I, 1) was partially restored on a level patch of high ground. The ruins next to it and lower down are believed to belong to a temple of Artemis (Fig. I, 2).

At the foot of the hill, amidst groves of olive-trees, the following buildings have been restored: the theatre (Fig. I, 3), which was used as an Odeon or a place where students were taught rhetoric, and the stadium (Fig. I, 4), which retains only its sphendone and the seats of the presiding judges. The gymnasium, which was situated NE of the stadium, housed an important library of rhetoric. Gymnasiums were centres not only for physical exercise, but also for cultivation of the intellect: Strabo reports that it was adorned with as many artworks, as was the Dionysium, a sort of picture gallery.

The orator and sophist Aelius Aristides, in his speech on rebuilding Rhodes after the earthquake of AD 155, provides useful information on the city. He says it was "theatre-like", with buildings which faced east and gently descended the slope of Agios Stefanos. Its streets were broad (some reached the impressive width of 16.5 m), straight, and ran through the whole town, forming a regular grid. (To date archaeologists have located 80 such streets.) At first their surface was nothing more than tamped-down earth, but after the earthquake in 227/6 BC, they were paved with a mixture of sand, gravel and potsherds, held together with lime. In the second century AD this was replaced with slabs of local grey marble. Certain roads had large masonry conduits for water and sewage; some were hollowed out of the rock.

At first every block of buildings had three houses of identical dimensions. Houses that occupied whole blocks, with mosaic floors, wall-paintings, reception areas, baths, bathing-pools, etc., give some idea of the wealth and opulence the city had attained by the second and first centuries BC. Most of the houses that have been excavated date from this era of prosperity, from the second century BC up to early Roman times. The most common type of house is one with an atrium surrounded by a type of peristyle where one row of columns was higher than the rest, known as "Rhodian", as mentioned by the Roman architect Marcus Vitruvius Pollio in his *Architecture*.

Around this atrium the rooms and auxiliary areas were arranged. When such

Ruins next to the temple of Apollo, believed to belong to a temple of Artemis

buildings had an upper story, this usually contained the bedrooms and the women's apartments, or gynaeconitis. The sanitary facilities were located on the side of the house facing the road, so that they could easily be connected to the sewer system. Cellars were used to store and preserve foodstuffs. The suburbs of the ancient city were destroyed by the inhabitants themselves the moment they learned of Mithri-

The partially restored temple of Pythian Apollo, on the acropolis of ancient Rhodes

dates' impending attack! Unfortunately, apart from a few remnants of foundations of walls, houses, ancient streets and sewage conduits, every trace of the ancient city was built over in the 16th century.

As one would expect, the ancient city was embellished with important public and private buildings and splendid temples. Pliny counted several theatres, academies and other public buildings and, apart from the Colossus, 100 smaller colossi, together with 3,000 other statues. The remains of potteries, bronze workshops, and casting pits used in making the statues have been discovered in various parts of the town.

The agora (Fig. I, 10) and the "deigma" (= a building complex with stoas, for commercial activities) of ancient Rhodes, as described by Diodorus, lie under the middle part of the medieval town. In what is now the Square of the Evreon Martiron (Jewish Martyrs) stood the ancient city's second gymnasium, one stade (approx. 200 m) in length. Today it has been identified with the Ptolemaeum, an imposing edifice built in honour of Rhodes' benefactor King Ptolemy after the earthquake of 227/6 BC. The Dionysium must have been located in the lower part of town.

Other finds include ruins of buildings belonging to the sanctuary of Demeter (NE edge of the ancient city, Fig. I, 15), ruins of the Aesculapium (SW of the medieval town, Fig. I, 9) and between the commercial and naval harbours remains of the Doric temple of Aphrodite (Fig. I, 13)

Rock tombs at Karakonero

dating from the third century BC. In addition, an important sanctuary (Fig. I, 7), a late Hellenic altar and a foundry for casting colossal bronze statues were discovered in Diagoridon Street, and a sanctuary or public building with a stoa (Fig. I, 8) at the intersection of T. Sofouli and Himaras Streets. The great theatre must have been near the city wall. The sites of the Prytaneum and the Buleuterium have not been identified.

Near the seaward wall there was probably a sanctuary of the Egyptian goddess Isis: the commercial ties between the two peoples were conducive to the worship of foreign deities. It is even said that during Mithridates' siege, the appearance of the goddess' statue above the walls was enough to put the enemy to flight! (From an inscription it has been established that many other Egyptian and Phrygian deities were worshipped.)

The existence of three natural harbours, which provided a haven for ships in all types of weather, even before the city was founded, was one of the main reasons this site was chosen for the city. The five ancient ports – three are still in use today – had large sheds where ships could be hauled up and stored) and shipyards with drydocks. Present-day Mandraki was the site of the "small harbour", the ancient city's naval port. From Diodorus we learn that, in case of attack, the mouth of the harbour could be closed off with chains. It was forbidden for foreigners to enter its installations, on pain of death! Today's harbour, the "great harbour" of antiquity, has been in continuous use and has always had direct communication with the marketplace. The harbour in Akandia Bay served as a second port. Nearby were found a section of the ancient wall, altar bases and a temple dedicated to Poseidon of Growth (he who fertilises, who produces, Fig. I, 14). Of the other two harbours, one was located on the south side of the city, in the Zefiros area, where a section of the mole can be seen, and the other on the west side, near the Grand Hôtel.

The necropolis of the ancient city extended outside the walls and occupied vast area of over three kilometres south of the city (because the ancient Greeks never disinterred their dead). The oldest graves were in the form of pit-tombs, with a peaked or horizontal roof of porous stone. There were no valuable grave goods, and no particular ornamentation, apart from a stele of porous stone or marble. The city's prosperity in Hellenistic times led to the construction of imposing monumental complexes of tombs, hollowed out of the rock, which accommodated up to 100 burials. Steles or altars were erected over the tombs.

The most wealthy families had grand mausoleums built. Alongside burial, cremation of the dead was also practised; their ashes were placed in clay urns or stone ossuaries, for which special niches were carved out of or built into the tombs.

A variety of burial items accompanied the dead to their final resting place, including of course the obolus, or death-penny, to pay Charon to ferry them to Hades.

The quality of life in ancient Rhodes was on a par with that of Athens. Strabo preferred Rhodes to Rome or Alexandria. Small everyday objects, jewellery and toilet articles, expensive vases, and silver and glass vessels decorated with an impressive variety of themes show how wealthy the ancient Rhodians were. Both the sophist Athenaeus (AD 170-230, *Deipnosophists*) and the author Lynceus give us information on the Rhodian banquet, a custom that was particularly well-loved during Hellenistic times. The guests, crowned with myrtle or ivy, met in the andron (reception room) and ate lying on couches. Their discussions, on philosophical or erotic topics, were accompanied by poetry recitations, games of chance, or even theatrical or acrobatic performances. The sambyctistriae lent a note of gaiety to

Near present-day Mandraki is the "small harbour", the ancient city's naval harbour

In the Archaeological Museum's two-story colonnade, do not miss the altars, sepulchral monuments and the portion of the bas relief from the Roman tetrapylon (at left).

the atmosphere by playing the sambyce, a triangular four-stringed musical instrument like a harp. Dancing girls performed local dances, so scantily dressed that they looked almost naked. The banquet followed, consisting of a variety of dishes, such as fish, honeyed dough-cakes, and figs. The wine that flowed at these hearty repasts was of the kind that brings sweet dreams, and it was served either watered, or chilled, or flavoured with herbs (myrrh, anise, saffron, etc.). Wine was one of the island's most important products for export.

When Rhodes became a Roman province, the occupying forces, who always looked with envy on anything that brought recognition to a rival city, did not erect any public buildings or private dwellings. They merely paved a main thoroughfare that ran to the south from Mandraki, and lined it with colonnades. In the third century AD, they built a triumphal tetrapylon (Fig. I, 12) over the ruined sheds in the naval harbour.

Atop its square columns they placed, as was their custom, slabs decorated in bas relief. A large marble pediment with figures in bas relief found in the medieval town is believed to have been part of a Roman Nymphaeum (Fig. I, 11) of the 3rd century AD.

Sports in Ancient Rhodes

The ancient Greeks put physical exercise on a par with intellectual pursuits for young people. The only prerequisite was that one had to be a free citizen and be well off financially. Many important Rhodian athletes made a name for themselves, but it was the members of the Diagoridae family who reaped more laurels than any other victor in the Tlepolemia or the Panhellenic Olympic Games. Diagoras, his sons Damagetus, Acusilaus and Dorieus, and his grandsons Eucleus and Peisirhodus – Olympic victors every one – are said to have been members of the Eratides clan, descendants of Heracles. Statues were erected to them in the temple of Zeus in Olympia.

The most famous of all was Diagoras, son of Damagetus. His mother was the daughter of Aristomenes, King of Messenia, who came to live in Ialysia after the Second Messenian War (685-668 BC). Diagoras was a giant of a man (2.2 meters tall, according to Pindar). He went in for sports, first because he placed great importance on physical exercise and second because he did not want to get involved in politics or with the Athenians. He took part in all four of the biggest Panhellenic games (at Olympia, Isthmia, Nemea and Pythia), brought glory not only to himself but to his mother city as well, and became a symbol of athletics.

When he won the pugilistic contest in the 79th Olympics in 464 BC, Diagoras invited Pindar to the island, who sang the praises of the Diagoridae in his *7th Olympic Ode*. It was written in gold letters on a marble stele which was built into the wall of the temple of Lindian Athena. For the 83rd Olympiad, by then an old man, Diagoras, accompanied his sons Damagetus and Acusilaus to Olympia (448 BC). Lost in thought, he did not realise his sons had been victorious until the cheers and acclamations of the crowd brought him back to reality and the man next to him told him two youths from Rhodes had won. After the victors were crowned, his sons took him up on their shoulders and carried him, wearing the crown of olive, around the stadium, while the spectators extolled the fortunate father. One Spartan even jumped into the arena, kissed Diagoras, and said, "Die now, Diagoras. What else do you have to look forward to? Going up Mt. Olympus and becoming a god?" And in fact, as he passed the statue of Victory his weak old heart was unable to stand so much emotion and it stopped beating.

In 432 BC, his other son, Dorieus, added another victory to his historic family's record, this time in the pancratium. In 431 BC the disastrous Peloponnesian War began, and Dorieus, a broadly educated man with opinions on the political problems of his age, waited for the right moment to help his city escape from the harsh rule of the Athenians. In 428 BC he was once again victorious in the Olympic Games. A year later, Dorieus and his nephew Peisirhodus took the side of the Spartans. The uprising was unsuccessful and the rebels were forced to seek asylum in Thurium in order to avoid the death penalty (425 BC). In 424 BC, now a resident of Thurium, Dorieus won the pancratium at Olympia for the third time. Finally, the Rhodians, on Dorieus' urging, rose up in 411 BC, after Sparta's victory in Syme; Dorieus was one of those taking part. That same year he brought them together at the sanctuary of Lindian Athena, where it was decided to unite the three cities into one large one. Dorieus was involved in the political, military and even the technical preparations for founding the new city. In 408 BC, on his way back from Thurium, he was taken captive by the Athenian general Phanothenes.

The Athenians were infuriated with Dorieus. But when the general assembly of citizens met, seeing such a renowned man and noble antagonist a prisoner, it

Marble head of an athlete, possibly a work of Lysippus and his pupils (Rhodes Archaeological Museum)

freed him without punishment, and Dorieus never again fought against the Athenians!

Aside from Dorieus who was in the Peloponnese at the time, the whole Diagoridae clan was wiped out by revolutionary democrats in 396 BC. Dorieus himself, the inspirer and creator of the city of Rhodes, met with a tragic, inglorious end, when the enraged Spartans arrested and executed him.

Another descendant of the aristocratic line of the Diagoridae was Callipateira. As Pausanias relates (Book VI), the laws of the times forbade the fair sex to watch the games, as the athletes competed naked and insisted that the Helians throw violators of the rule over Mt. Typaea! (The same punishment awaited any woman who crossed the Alpheios River on the days when it was forbidden!) Women could congratulate the Olympic victor only after his glorious return to his city, when part of the city wall was torn down to let him pass.

But that was not enough for Callipateira. After the death of her husband Callianactas died, she dressed as a gymnast and entered the stadium, in order to watch her relatives take part in the games.

25

Pausanias says that, in her enthusiasm over the victory of her son or nephew, she began to jump for joy and tore her clothes off. When her deception was discovered, no one could take action against the daughter of Diagoras, sister of three Olympic victors (Dorieus, Damagetus and Acusilaus) and mother of another two (Eucleus and Peisirhodus). The judges forgave her, but from that time on even the gymnasts had to attend naked!

Letters in Ancient Rhodes

From ancient times, Rhodes was the birthplace of poets and men of the arts and letters. Her contribution to the intellectual life and art of the Greek world was a significant one. Moreover, Rhodes was one of the seven cities which claimed to be Homer's birthplace.

The epic poet Peisandrer wrote his epic *Heracleia* (late 7th century BC), where he describes the life and works of the leader Heracles. Cleobulus, son of Euagoras and tyrant of Lindus (early 6th century BC), one of the seven sages, wrote poems and riddles in his 300 epics. His best-known maxim was "everything in moderation". A tyrant for 40 years, he organised Lindus' internal policy, reformed its economy, carried out public works and built or restored the sanctuary of Lindian Athena in the following way: young children went from house to house carrying an artificial swallow and sang the "swallow's song" to collect money. [Athenaeus the sophist in his *Deipnosophists* attributes the swallow's song to Cleobulus. This custom lives on today in the song of Lazarus.] According to the author Diogenes Laertius (AD 200), Cleobulus offered asylum to his friend and fellow sophist Solon during the time Peisistratus was tyrant. His daughter was a poet who wrote riddles in hexameter.

Other poets of that era were the comic poet Antheus from Lindus, the sceptic lyric poet Timocreon from Ialysus (early 5th century BC) and Anaxandrides from Camirus (early 4th century BC). The poet, philologist and orator Apollonius (later Rhodius, 3rd century BC) took refuge in Rhodes when he was forced to leave Alexandria or Naucratis. He taught on the island, and to honour him the Rhodians made him a citizen of the island: this shows their appreciation of art. One of his works is the epic *Argonautica* (5,834 verses).

Panaetius, son of Nicagorus from Camirus (185-110 BC) was a great philosopher. He was the principal founder of the Middle Stoa (philosophical school of the ancient Stoics). He became a leading figure of the Stoic School in Athens (whose followers stressed the interdependence of man and nature). When the Athenians honoured him with the right to become an Athenian citizen, he rejected their suggestion, saying that one mother-city was enough for him. Ecaton of Rhodes and Poseidonius of Apameia in Syria (135-51 BC) were pupils of his; the latter became a citizen of Rhodes and taught there. Orators who taught in Rhodes were Apollonius the Soft and Apollonius Molon from Alabanda in Asia Minor. In 99 BC, the Lindian philologist and historian Timachidas, son of Agesitimus, wrote the famous *Chronicle of the Sanctuary of Lindos*.

The island's reputation as a centre of learning was already well-established in antiquity. Moreover, as it occupied a coveted position among the cultural capitals of the ancient world, Rhodes had all the necessary prerequisites for men of intellect to settle there. The philosopher Aristippus of Cyrene, a pupil of Socrates, the philosopher and mathematician Eudemus of Rhodes, a pupil of Aristotle, the exiled Athenian orator Aeschines (who founded Rhodes' school of oratory in the 4th century BC), and the astronomer Hipparchus of Nicaea in Bithynia all taught in Rhodes. In the field of intellect, Rhodes rivalled the most important centres for higher learning during the 2nd, but particularly during the 1st century BC, and became a pole of attraction for many eminent Romans (Tiberius Gracchus, Scipio Aemilianus Africanus the Younger, Cicero, Julius Caesar, Pompey, Lucretius, Brutus, Cassius, Cato the Younger, Mark Antony, etc.) who disseminated Greek culture in the West.

Marine Law in Ancient Rhodes

Legislative power in ancient Rhodes was greatly admired by the Romans. Shipping on Rhodes, which was a hub of communications by sea, began to develop in the 8th century BC, but only reached a zenith after the decline of Athenian hegemony. The strong commercial ties and the course of colonisation on which the seafaring people of Rhodes had embarked throughout the then known world impelled them to enact marine laws quite early on. In Rhodes, the first written marine law of its kind in the history of the world was created, and it came to be respected by all the ancient states. From Hellenistic times up to the present it has constituted the basis of international marine legislation.

The Roman Emperor Caius Caesar or Octavian (63 BC-14 AD, to whom the Senate awarded the honorary imperial title of "Augustus" = holy, respected) used certain elements of Rhodian law (Lex Rhodia) to write Roman law. After studying it, the Roman Emperor Antoninus Pius (AD 86-161) said characteristically: "I may rule the world, but Rhodian Law rules the sea!"

Today we have no satisfactory information on the provisions of Rhodian Law. Be that as it may, one of the matters it regulated was the question of "common average" (in the collection of laws of the Byzantine Emperor Justinian *Pandectes*, 24.2, de lege rhodia de jactu): common average is the damages, the contingent expenses, even the loss of the whole cargo incurred

intentionally to save the ship (or the cargo) in a situation of danger at sea, provided the sought-after beneficial result has ensued. In addition, common average includes wages and victualling expenses in case of delay due to war or repairs.

Rhodes' marine law should not be confused with the Marine Law of the Rhodians, which is a private Byzantine collection of the 7th-9th centuries AD; also known as the "pseudorhodian law" it is primarily a codification of nautical customs and habits.

The Arts in Ancient Rhodes

On the basis of the archaeological finds which have come to light so far, we cannot speak of an art that is purely Rhodian; the island followed the general artistic currents of the Hellenic world. But the introduction of local factors helps us distinguish works with Rhodian features. Moreover, we should not forget the island's mythological tradition, which relates that the Telchines, the island's first inhabitants, were brilliant artists, and that later its protectress, the

Black-figure amphora from the grave of an adolescent (Drakidis) in the ancient necropolis of Ialysus (Rhodes Archaeological Museum)

goddess Athena, gave the Rhodians the gift of being outstanding artists. Unfortunately, only a very few works of famous sculptors and painters have been preserved, and even fewer remain in the place where they were made.

There are many potsherds, a few intact decorative vases, and small sections of wall-paintings from the excavations in Ialysus (Trianda) where the influence of Minoan art on the island's painters can be seen. In addition to the pottery of the late Minoan period, a few works of miniature art found among grave goods are evocative of similar works from the rest of Greece. Pottery of the early Geometric period was strongly influenced by contemporary Attic pottery. From 750 BC on, a geometric style peculiar to Rhodes began to develop, at least with regard to decoration. Plastic art (wooden statues, clay figurines,

The famous 5th-century BC stele of Crito and Timarista, from the necropolis of ancient Camirus (Rhodes Archaeological Museum)

etc.) also followed the course of development in Greece as a whole.

Beginning in the 7th century BC, geometric austerity disappeared from the artistic spirit of the age and an "orientalising" tendency with Corinthian influences took hold. The last types of archaic pottery of the 6th century BC were "Phicelloura ware", pottery discovered on Mt. Phicelloura, near ancient Camirus, and pottery in the "Brulia" style, also from the 6th century BC, discovered at the Brulia site, on Rhodes' southern tip. Early in the third century BC, pottery appeared which belonged to the "Western Clitys" category (which originated in Athens), along with polychrome hydriae (mainly cinerary urns) of the "Hadra" type (from the Alexandrian graveyard of the same name). From the first century BC on, potters' workshops used moulds to mass produce pottery and figurines.

The influence of the orientalising style can also be seen in bronze work (vessels) and in miniature art (jewellery). Works of archaic plastic art are small in size and Ionic in character. At the end of the 5th century BC we have an example of purely Rhodian art, the grave stele in low relief of "Crito and Timarista".

The School of Rhodes, which was to flourish for three centuries to come, was established around the 4th century BC by the sculptor Lysippus of Sicyon. He lived in the court of Alexander the Great, and created the famous colossal bronze "Chariot of the Sun". (Around the same time, the city of Rhodes dedicated a similar gilded chariot at Delphi. Constantine the Great carried it from Rome to Constantinople. In 1204 it adorned St. Mark's in Venice. In 1797 Napoleon took it to Paris, but after his downfall it was once again transported to Venice!) Various other foreign artists were called to Rhodes, among them the painter Parrasius of Ephesus, the Athenian sculptor Bryaxis, the painters Apelles of Cos, portrait painter of Alexander the

Great, and Protogenes of Caunus in Caria, whose paintings adorned the Dionysium.

According to Pliny, the "Ialysus" was his work. It was a painting which took either 7 or 11 years to complete and depicted the hero Ialysus as a hunter with his panting dog. When Demetrius the Besieger conquered the areas outside the city walls, the Rhodians sent delegates to plead with him not to destroy Protogenes' works. Demetrius answered that he would rather burn the portrait of his father, Antigonus, painted by Protogenes himself! When they met, Demetrius asked the artist how he could be indifferent to his mother island and his own life. Protogenes replied that he knew the king was battling against the Rhodians, not against art! It is said that Demetrius stationed a guard outside Protogenes' workshop, visited him often to admire his works, and finally forgot his original purpose of conquering Rhodes! One of his well-known works was the "Resting Satyr", a painting depicting a satyr holding pipes, leaning on a column, atop which a partridge was perched. Strabo says that the bird was so beautifully painted that no one paid any attention to the main subject. Moreover, breeders of partridges brought young birds to see the painted one, and the noise they made a terrible racket! Finally, Protogenes asked for permission from the custodians of the temenos to remove the partridge from the painting.

We can glean information on painting and interior decoration of Rhodian homes between the 4th century BC and early Roman times from the frescos and important mosaic floors in nymphaea, tombs and sanctuaries; they are characterised by their technique, polychrome representations, and rendering of detail. One such outstanding mosaic is that depicting a mask of the New Comedy. Among the large mosaic floors are the "Centaur" mosaic, which, according to the ancient author Lucian (of Samosata, Syria, AD 120-180), was created by the painter Zeuxis

around the end of the 5th century BC, the "Bellerophon" mosaic (from the same house), and the "Triton" mosaic, possibly by the same artist. Of later date is the "Griffon" mosaic (in the Rhodes Museum). A famous mosaic of Roman times is the "Rape of Europa".

Rhodes' school of sculpture has many famous works to show, such as the renowned "Victory of Samothrace", now a jewel in the collection of the Louvre! This work is attributed by present-day scholars to Pythocritus, son of Timochares. Evidence of its Rhodian origin are the base of the statue depicting a ship, a common theme in Rhodian sculpture – it showed that the Lindians were a pre-eminently seafaring people – and the Lardos marble from which it was sculpted. It was dedicated by the Rhodians to the sanctuary of the Cabiri in Samothrace on the occasion of the victory of the Rhodian admiral Eudamus over Antioch III (the Great) of Syria (190 BC). Another work of Pythocritus is the partially ruined relief of a ship's stern at the entrance to the acropolis of Lindus; it also served as a base for a statue.

Hellenistic marble statue of Zeus or Sarapis (Rhodes Archaeological Museum)

The groups found in Sperlonga cave in Italy are attributed to the Rhodian sculptors Polydorus, Athenodorus and Agesander; they are works that demonstrate the esteem in which Rhodian plastic arts were held in the milieu of the Roman emperors. Best known is the Hellenistic "Laocoön" group, dating from the 2nd/1st century BC (height 2.42 m), which was bought by Pope Julius II and is now in the Vatican! According to Pliny, it was carried to Rome in the first century AD, as a gift from the Rhodians to the Emperor Titus. It was discovered in 1506 in a field in which an inhabitant of Rome was digging, and it caused so much admiration among contemporary artists that not even the great Renaissance artist Michelangelo Buonarotti (1475-1564) would agree to restore the work, out of fear that he might not be able to match the quality of the original! Laocoön was a Trojan priest of Poseidon. In the *Aeneid*, the great Roman epic poet Vergil (70-19 BC) says that Laocoön forbade the Trojans to bring the Trojan horse into the city. So the gods, who were on the side of the Greeks, sent two adders from Tenedos which killed Laocoön and his sons.

A somewhat later group in the baroque style was that of "Dirce", which showed the sons of Zeus and Antiope, Zethus and Amphion, punishing Dirce — for having pursued their mother to Mt. Cithaeron —, by tying her to the horns of a wild bull, which killed her as it ran madly about. It was sculpted in Rhodes by Apollonius and Tauriscus from Tralleis in Asia Minor. A variant copy of the group was made late in the third century AD. This copy was discovered in excavations carried out by Pope Paul III between 1540 and 1560; the sculptor Giambattista della Porta unhesitatingly restored it. It is the "Pharnesian Bull", now in the Museo Nazionale in Naples.

The zenith of bronze statuary in Rhodes was reached with the famous "Colossus", a great achievement of its time

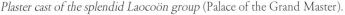

Plaster cast of the splendid Laocoön group (Palace of the Grand Master).

30

and fifth among the seven wonders of the ancient world. Its association with the island was so strong that during the Middle Ages the Rhodians were renamed "Colossaeans" and the Italian archbishop in charge of the Order of the Knights "Archiepiscopus Colossensis". The huge bronze statue depicted the sun god Helios (or the god Apollo, according to some). It was erected as a trophy after Demetrius' siege was successfully warded off, and dedicated to Helios. It was 60 cubits (approximately 34 m) in height, but nothing else is known about its appearance, apart from the face, which is depicted on ancient coins. It took several people to gird its thumb, Pliny wrote, when he saw it lying on the ground after the earthquake! Its construction took 12 years (304-292 BC), and cost 300 talents (1 talent = 26 kg. of gold), a sum collected by the Rhodians by selling off the spoils and the siege artillery left behind by Demetrius to erect a monument in memory of the naval battle of 304 BC.

Experts' opinions are divided with regard to the creator and the situation of the Colossus. Pliny tells us that it was the work of Chares of Lindus, pupil of Lysippus, but the lyric poet Simonides of Ceos and Strabo say that it was completed by Laches, a contemporary of Chares. The statue stood upright for 56 years; it was visible from the sea and from all the harbours of the ancient city, and was used as a reference point in surveying. Savants in the Middle Ages and in later times created a myth that had the Colossus standing astride the entrance to the harbour, with one foot on the site of the lazaretto and the other on the site of the fortress of Agios Nikolaos or the lighthouse tower. Ships supposedly passed between its legs. It is more probable that the gigantic statue stood within the enclosure of the temple of the god, where the Castello stands today. The engineer Philon Byzantius and the Vice Chancellor of the Order of the

Knights, Guillaume Caoursin, agree that it stood with its legs together on a marble base on the site of the fortress of Agios Nikolaos (but this theory is untenable, because, according to the law of gravity, it would have toppled over).

The general and historian Polybius the Megalopolitan (ca. 200-125/120 BC, Book V, 88-90) relates that when the great earthquake of 227/6 BC struck, the Colossus levelled 30 houses as it fell, along with part of the city walls and the dockyards. Strabo adds that the legs of the statue cracked and, unable to hold up the weight of the body, it collapsed. But because to Philon it seemed impossible that the Rhodians would have left the pieces of their statue scattered on the ground for the next 9 centuries without being inconvenienced by them, he claimed that the sculptor skilfully placed huge rocks in the legs to counterbalance the weight of the body, and stood

The way the Colossus is usually represented, from the book Monuments de Rhodes *by Colonel Rottiers*

The small Church of Agii Apostoli in Lindos was built to commemorate the visit of the Apostle Paul to the island.

it on its feet again. This theory, too, seems absurd today, as the dimensions of the statue would have made such an operation impossible. The most likely theory is that the Colossus was never repaired, out of superstition and respect for the prophecy of the Sibyls (an oriental name given to godlike female figures in possession of powers of prophecy), who had foreseen that great evils would befall the city if the pieces of the Colossus were moved.

In AD 653, Arabs from the Land of Moab conquered Rhodes and sold the pieces of the Colossus to a Jewish merchant of Edessa in Syria. It was destined to be melted down in later times to make weapons. According to Byzantine texts, 900 camels were needed to transport it! Pliny mentions that there were 100 smaller Colossi on the island!

From Chares of Lindos on, sculptors (Philiscus, Heliodorus, Boethus) worked mainly in bronze. Splendid examples of the rococo style are the excellent bronze "Sleeping Eros" by an unknown artist of the middle Hellenistic period, now in the Metropolitan Museum in New York, and the head of a "Gaul", in the Cairo museum!

The use of glass (a synthetic material made of sand, soda and lime) began late in the third millennium BC in Western Asia, northern Mesopotamia and Egypt. The oldest (3rd-2nd century BC) known glass-works in the Greek area was found in Rhodes; it produced fine vessels and jewellery.

Deinocrates, the city-planner and personal architect of Alexander the Great, is said to have come from Rhodes. He designed Alexandria (331 BC) and the tomb of Hephaestion in Babylon, and wanted to transform Mt. Athos into a gigantic statue of Alexander, holding a city of 10,000 in his left hand! In addition, Alexander the Great made the Rhodians the keepers of his treasure, and based the policy of the city of Alexandria on Rhodian models. The islet outside the harbour of Alexandria was named Antirrhodon (= on a par with Rhodes).

Byzantine and Medieval Times

Christianity spread to the island early on, thanks to the visit of the Apostle Paul in AD 57 during his third voyage from Miletus to Syria. That marked the beginning of Church of Rhodes, which after the fourth century became the Metropolis of the Aegean islands.

In 279, under the Roman Emperor Diocletian (AD 284-305), Rhodes became the capital of the Province of the Islands (Provincia Insularum), which was set up for better protection from pirates. The island was unable to regain its former prosperity and continued its gradual decline. It did not cease to be regarded as an important harbour, however. It was reduced to a mere Roman Province, experienced the wrath of Enceladus (the powerful earthquake of AD 155, which destroyed half the city – the author and archaeologist Edouard C. Biliotti informs us that it was rebuilt by the Roman Emperor Antoninus Pius – the earthquake of 344-5 recorded by the Byzantine chronicler Georgus Cedrinus, and the earthquake of 515, during the reign of the Byzantine Emperor Anastasius I, which claimed thousands of

Excavations currently under way in Panetiou and Apellou Streets have brought to light medieval buildings and a section of the Byzantine wall (7th-13th centuries).

victims), and was plundered by the Goths in 269.

In early Byzantine times, the Rhodians, unable to repair the damage caused by the earthquake of AD 515 in their vast city, restricted it to the area around the commercial harbour (three-quarters of the ancient city remained outside the new settlement). When the Roman Emperor Theodosius divided up the Roman Empire in 395, Rhodes became part of the Eastern Roman Empire. (Information on that era is scant, as Byzantine chroniclers were only concerned with disasters and invasions.)

In 687 Rhodes became part of the Theme of Carabesianae or Cibyraeotae. Despite many precautions, it was repeatedly attacked by pirates (in 469-470 from Isauria in Asia Minor, in 620 by Chosroes II and his Persians, in 653 by Arabs from the Land of Moab, and in 807 by the Seljuk Caliph of the Abbasids in Baghdad, Arun al Rashid and his successor Mamun).

In the 11th century, the Byzantine Emperor Nicephorus Phocas liberated the Aegean from the Arabs, but opened the way for incursions from the West, as he permitted Venice and the other Italian maritime cities to carry on trade with the Levant. The Byzantine Emperor Alexius Comnenus I granted even more privileges to the Venetians (1082), to secure their assistance in his struggles against the Nor-

mans. The towns of Genoa and Pisa later obtained similar privileges. Rhodes was occupied for three years by the Turkish pirate Caha, and suffered Byzantine persecution in 1092.

The eight great campaigns of the Middle Ages, which started out from the West to free the Holy Land from the Muslims, were known as the Crusades. During the First Crusade in 1096, the Crusaders spent the winter in Rhodes on their way to Palestine. In 1124, and in general every time one or another of the Byzantine Emperors took away the privileges of the Venetians, the latter replied by sacking the islands. During the Third Crusade, the King of France Philip II Augustus and the King of England Richard I the Lionhearted put in at Rhodes and recruited mercenarics (1191).

In 1204 the members of the Fourth Crusade took Constantinople and signed a treaty with the Venetians dividing up the Byzantine Empire. The islands devolved to the Venetians, with the exception of

The loggia of St. John before the siege of Rhodes
(*Rottiers*, Monuments de Rhodes)

Rhodes, which was declared independent by its governor Leon Gavalas. When his brother and successor Ioannes sided with Byzantium at Nicomedia against the Latins, the Genoans seized the opportunity to occupy the island (1248).

Two years later it was liberated and became part of the Byzantine Empire of Nicaea. When Michael Palaeologus VIII occupied Constantinople, he ceded Rhodes to his brother Ioannes (1261-1275). After 1278, it belonged, together with the other nearby islands, to the Genoan corsair I. Del Cavo, and from 1282 to 1307 to another Genoan, A. Moresco, for his services in the struggles of the Palaeologi against the Turks and the Catalans.

The Era of the Knights – The Turkish Occupation

When Moresco was taken prisoner, the shrewd, farsighted Grand Master of the Order of the Knights of St. John, Foulques de Villaret, who had set his sights on the island as a base for his itinerant order, acquired it with the help of its last Genoan owner, Admiral Vinolo da Vignoli, on August 15, 1309.

At the end of the 11th century, merchants from Amalfi in Italy had asked the Caliph of Egypt to allow them to maintain an inn/hospital in Acra, Palestine for those who made the long, dangerous pilgrimage to the Holy Land. But before a century had passed, their purely monastic, charitable, ministrant duties had taken on a military character, and they began to participate in the struggles against the Muslims. In 1291 the "Order of the Knights of St. John of Jerusalem" was expelled from Palestine by the Mamelukes and retreated temporarily to Limassol in Cyprus.

Initially the Knights took the fortress of Faraklos and then of Filerimo (1306). Three years later they conquered the city of Rhodes and were renamed the "Knights of Rhodes". During this new period, Rhodes was transformed into a bastion of the Christian world against the Muslims' desire for conquest, and was repeatedly attacked by the Egyptians and Turks. From Rhodes, the Knights sallied forth on the military campaigns of the Western countries in the East; they also offered protection to fugitives.

The Order ruled the island for 213 years. Because of the difference in dogma, there were conflicts, mainly on religious matters (recognition of the spiritual leadership of the Pope, refusal of entry to the Orthodox bishop), but these were overcome in the face of the Turkish menace. In the countryside, the feudal lord was master of the stronghold and the land was worked by the serfs (the common people). Sailors became slaves in the galleys. All these things caused the economy to stagnate.

The Order's patron was St. John the Baptist. Its members were known as "infermarii", and according to their social class were divided into: a) knights of justice, of aristocratic stock, who held leading posts in administration and in the military; b) chaplains, with religious duties; and c) serving brothers or fighting squires, attendant upon the knights. They came from Roman Catholic countries and provinces of Europe (Provence, Auvergne, France,

Italy, Spain, Germany and England), and were organised in seven "Tongues", or national groups [finally eight, because under Grand Master Pedro Raimondo Zacosta (1461-1467), Spain was divided into Aragon and Castile]. The general religious head of the Tongues was the Grand Master (Magnus Magister), elected by the General Chapter (Capitulum Generale) for life – a total of 19 Grand Masters served as leaders of the Order. The high administrative officials [the Grand Master and the legislative-disciplinary Chapter, consisting of the Bailiffs of the Tongues (Pillerii), elected only by the Knights] had its seat in the palace, whereas the rest of the officials of the eight Tongues lived in their respective quarters, known as the inn (auberge). The official language of the order was Latin in the beginning, and later French. Its standard was red with a large white cross in the middle. The Knights wore purple capes; their insigne was an octagonal white cross on the left side. They carried swords and wore gold spurs.

In 1310 the island was besieged by the Sultan Othoman, and later by his son Orhan. The Turkish Sultan Mahomet II the Conqueror (1430-1481) plundered Archangelos in 1457. In 1480 his envoy, the Greek renegade Mesih Pasha Palaeologus, laid siege to the harbour of Agios Stefanos (Trianda). The 15th Grand Master, Pierre d'Aubusson (1476-1503) managed to fend him off.

The inhabitants of the city whose homes were outside the city walls removed everything that could possibly have been of use to the enemy. They even tore down the churches, to be rebuilt after the battle was won. It is said that Mahomet, conqueror of Constantinople, died of disappointment when he was not able to take Rhodes!

The island was hard hit by the plague in 1498 (described in the poem by E. Limenitis tou Georgila The Plague of Rhodes). Repeated Turkish invasions dur-

In the Street of the Knights, on the facade of the small 14th-century Church of the Holy Trinity, there is a niche with a stone statue of the Virgin and Child.

ing the last 50 years of the rule of the Knights left the city and the countryside impoverished.

Under the 19th Grand Master, Philippe

Present-day Agiou Fanouriou Street (old medieval street). The bridge-like supports are to hold up the houses in case of an earthquake.

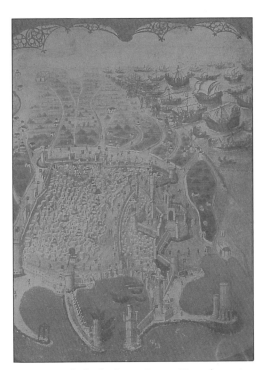

The siege of Rhodes by Mahomet II, as shown in a miniature in a 15th-century Codex by Caoursin, who was an eye-witness to the siege (Paris, Bibliotheque Nationale)

Villiers de l'Isle-Adam (1521-1522), Rhodes came under a violent attack by the Turkish Sultan Suleiman II the Magnificent (26 June 1522). The islanders put up a heroic resistance. They prevented the attackers from entering the castle by raining boiling oil, pitch, rocks, etc. down on them. The

The Gate of St. Athan was built up in 1531 by Suleiman himself, to prevent anyone else from entering and taking the city.

continued victories of the Knights would have forced the Sultan to raise the siege, as historians of the Order maintain, had the Bailiff of Castile, the Portuguese chancellor André d' Amaral not told him what a sorry state the besieged were in. When Villiers de l'Isle-Adam had been elected Grand Master, d'Amaral had threatened that he would be the last. But his treachery came to light, and the Knights sentenced him to death, quartered his body and hung it in the fortress for all to see, as was the custom in those times!

The Knights were forced to surrender the island on January 1, 1523, after securing their safe departure; along with about 5,000 islanders, they set sail for Crete and later moved to Malta. The Turks immediately began furious reprisals. They raped the women, demolished the churches and threw the sick out onto the streets. The remaining Rhodians formed certain movements to bring back the Knights, while the Knights with secret longing watched developments taking place on the island.

In theory, Suleiman forbade his soldiers to engage in plunder and rapine, to convert churches into mosques, to kidnap children and to forcibly convert the population to Islam. Nevertheless the Turkish presence in Rhodes was particularly harsh, in view of the fact that the island had not capitulated of its own free will, and also of the fact that it was the capital of the Vilayet (Provence) of the Archipelago. The numerous native population lived outside the castle, but people could remain inside to carry on their business from sunrise to sunset. Only the few members of the occupying force lived inside the castle (Turkish quarter), together with the Jewish population (Jewish quarter).

In 1533, Rhodes, Mytilene and Euboea were given as timars to the terrible pirate and Admiral of the Turkish fleet Khayr al-Din Barbarossa. In 1658, the Venetian Admiral Francesco Morosini launched an attack on the Turks of Rhodes.

When the Greek Revolution broke out in 1821, the island became a base for various operations by the Turks and their Egyptian allies. The members of the Friendly Society – a secret organisation established in Odessa in 1816 to organise the armed struggle of the Greeks against the Turks – were immediately thrown into jail; economic and administrative privileges were abolished, and in general there was no leeway for reactions. In 1822 the Greek government discussed ceding Rhodes, Karpathos and Astipalea to the Knights, in exchange for moral and economic support – Napoleon Bonaparte had expelled them from Malta in 1797 – but this plan was never implemented.

When the new Greek state was set up, the islands of the Dodecanese were self-governing, except for Rhodes and Kos which were governed as Turkish provinces. Although in general the two peoples lived and worked together in peace, the Turks as a nation suffered periodic defeats which caused them to lash out at the Christian element. Heavy taxation, complete lack of education, natural disasters (earthquakes in 1851, 1856, 1862; fire in 1876) further sapped the island's strength.

During the Cretan Revolution of 1896, the Ottoman government began bringing Greek-speaking Muslim settlers to Rhodes from Crete. Tension was created between the new settlers and the locals, and Konstantinos Alexandridis, who served as Metropolitan from 1893 to 1900, and the Philhellene Ottoman prefect of the Archipelago Ambedin Pasha worked diligently to avoid an uprising.

The First and Second Period of Italian Occupation – German and British Occupation

The new subjugation introduced by the Italian occupation after the Balkan Wars of 1912 caused the Dodecanese to com-

Priest of Arnitha with his family (from the book Lindos IV, *by Wriedt and Pentz, National Museum of Denmark)*

pletely cease to exist as an administrative entity. Italy, which declared war on Turkey in order to take Tripoli, Libya and thus relieve its demographic problem, decided first of all to occupy all the islands off the coast of Asia Minor, to prevent Turkey from sending help and force her to sign a peace pact. On May 4, the Italians landed in Kallithea and took the Turks prisoner. In the occupation proclamation issued by General Giovanni Ameglio, they assured the islanders that they would soon have an autonomous government, thus raising Greek hopes of having their nationality restored.

In the Treaty of Lausanne, signed in 1912, Turkey recognised Italy's domination of Libya, but the Dodecanese went to Turkey, a fact which caused panic among the islanders, who had welcomed the Italians as liberators and had openly expressed their opposition to the Turks. The petitions sent to European governments met with coolness and indifference, and the Italians, who had stayed behind to keep the Greeks from occupying the islands, took harsh measures to crush the patriotic feelings of the islanders. When these facts were made public, the Italians were forced to cede the islands to Greece (agreement between the Italian Foreign Minister Esteri Tittoni and the Greek Prime Minister Eleftherios Venizelos) – all except for Rhodes, whose fate was to be decided in a plebiscite five years later. The terms of this agreement were not respected, and in accordance with the first Treaty (of Lausanne) Italy became master of the Dodecanese in 1923.

One Mario Lago was appointed governor of the island with absolute rights. The new political line (appointment of Italians to key positions in the Church and schools, mixed marriages, etc.) aimed at italianising the island. The truth is that during that period the Italians carried out public works by exploiting the local workforce. They developed archaeological sites (as they had the right to carry out excavations on the island) and laid the first foundations for promoting Rhodes as a tourist centre. Such works were primarily to their own benefit. In addition, all administrative and economic privileges which had been extended by the Turks were abolished, sectors of production went into decline, real estate and urban property devolved to the Italian government, and onerous taxation was imposed, without any corresponding social benefits. A fascist propaganda campaign was launched.

In 1936, the architect Cesare Maria de Vecchi, Minister of Education and a member of the fascist quadrumvirate, arrived on Rhodes. He ousted Lago, became governor of the island, and immediately issued decrees outlawing the use of the Greek language and making Italian mandatory. It was forbidden to raise the Greek flag, education was italianised (teaching of Greek history and geography was banned, and Greek teachers dismissed), and Greek printing-offices were closed down. When Italy occupied Ethiopia, Rhodes was turned into a virtual military camp.

Such was the prevailing atmosphere of de-hellenisation on the island, when Hitler invaded Greece and joined forces with the Italians. When war was declared, all of

The installations at the Kallithea hydropathic establishment, one of the island's many tourist infrastructure works

Rhodes' Greek citizens between the ages of 20 and 60 were imprisoned in the moat, where they were held in unsanitary conditions.

In 1943, after the arrest of the creator of fascism, dictator Benito Mussolini (1883-1945), the reins of government were taken up by the Italian Field-Marshal Pietro Badoglio, who surrendered to the Allies. When the Germans took Rome, they occupied Rhodes as well, and brutally annihilated the Italian troops there. Nor did Rhodes' Jews escape their fury. The German military headquarters was located in the Castle. Resistance fighters broadcast information to the Allies from Limeri cave near Monolithos.

On May 8, 1945, the Germans retreated, but the islanders were left in the throes of a terrible famine. On May 9, 1945, the British forces and emissaries from the Greek Sacred Band landed in Rhodes. Athanassios Kazoulis was appointed Rhodes' first Greek mayor. During the brief British presence, no major changes were made in the administration, as the British and Italians held key positions in political, judicial and administrative power. Nor did they arrange to implement some sort of programme to heal the economic wounds left by the Italo-German occupation.

The long-desired union of the Dodecanese with the rest of Greece came about on February, 1947, with the signing of a peace treaty between Italy and the Allies. The official ceremony of their incorporation was held in March, 1948.

Cultivation of olive-trees has been a basic occupation of the islanders through the ages (Asklipio Folklore Museum).

The monument to the members of the Sacred Band who fell in liberating the Aegean islands during World War II

Rhodes' medieval town is the only one of its kind in the world, enclosed within city walls, with arcaded passageways and winding lanes.

Of all the occupations of the city, that of the Knights has left the most indelible marks.

The Medieval Town Today

The most pleasant experience for today's visitor to the densely-inhabited town is to wander through its winding lanes, where he may happen upon covered passageways, Turkish wooden window-lattices, enclosed wooden balconies ("sahnissia") and mosques, Gothic churches or the Jewish synagogue. And even if he loses his way, he will feel the joy of discovery,

Figure II: *Street plan of the medieval town, based on a topographical map in* The Medieval Town of Rhodes and the Palace of the Grand Master, *by the noted ephor of Byzantine antiquities, Ilias Kollias.*

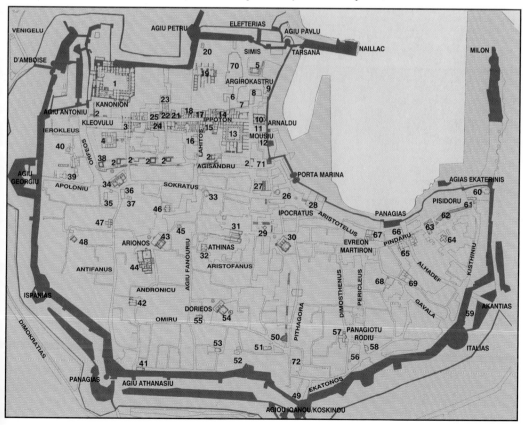

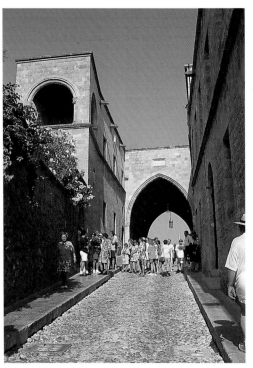

because this is a town of unlimited possibilities, where every nook and cranny has something important and unique to show.

Of all the foreign occupations of the town of Rhodes, the one which left the most indelible marks, despite its short duration, was that of the Knights. A few slender minarets and fountains remind us of the Turkish presence: the occupying forces did not need to add any buildings to those already in existence to meet their needs. The Italians made a major contribution to the town; their intervention cannot be regarded merely as restoration work, but rather as almost complete reconstruction.

In the beginning, the Byzantine city retained the ancient street grid, but the broad Hippodamian streets were gradually encroached upon, they ceased to be straight, and some became cul-de-sacs. The last time the medieval town was rebuilt was after the earthquake in 1481. The

Above: *A building dating from the time of the Knights, at the top of Ippoton Street, houses the Hellenic Organisation of Small and Medium-Sized Industries and Handicrafts (EOMMEX.)*
Below: *The town's towers, minarets and church bell-towers, lit by the rays of a summer sunset*

Of primary concern to the Knights during their two centuries of rule was strengthening the island's defences in every way possible.

walled city was laid out on three levels and divided into two parts: On the first level were the palace and the Church of St. John (10 m above sea level); on the second level were the Castle or Collachium, where the Knights lived, and on the third was the Hora (or Burgus or Burgum), where the Greek and Jewish burghers and merchants lived. This arrangement demonstrates the medieval ideas prevailing at that time and the strictly monarchic character of the order.

The Knights, who were almost continually besieged, built an amazing complex of walls, towers and other fortification works in the city and throughout the island, which they transformed into a huge fortress. The town's masterfully built walls, a representative example of defensive architecture, had a circumference of four kilometres; perpendicular or sloping down to the moat, their cores date back to Byzantine times. The Byzantine fortifications must have been begun after the earthquake of AD 515, and it is almost certain that the fortification of the Collachium took place late in the 7th century; the remaining areas were probably fortified later, due to limited economic resources. Indeed, they were probably of the same shape and size as the Knights' fortifications seen today. (In many streets in the medieval town, parts of the Byzantine fortification of the Collachium have been found, Fig. II, 2, 29.)

The walls were given their present form by the additions and improvements made by the Knights in the period between the sieges of 1480 and 1522, when Rhodes fell to the Ottoman Turks. When the Knights took Rhodes in 1309, they strengthened or repaired the stronghold using the existing building materials, erected the first gates and towers, and extended the landward wall. A second, inner defence wall separated the Castle from the town. In 1465 the enceinte was divided into 8 sections; the defence of each was allotted to one of the 8 tongues of the order. You can take the tour of the outer road which encircles the impressive walls, on Tuesday or Saturday at 2:45 pm from the Palace.

Under Giovanni Battista degl' Orsini (1467-1476), major works were undertaken to improve the island's defences. The brigadier and excellent engineer Pierre d'Aubusson took on the job of systematic reconstruction. He deepened the moat and increased its total width to 41 m (it never filled with water because it lies above sea level), strengthened the wall with bastions, converted the square towers into round ones, and erected a wall on the seaward side, where the Gate of St. Paul stands today. The wall here bore his coat of arms, as it did in 50 other places.

The visitor may enter the medieval town from one of ten gates (seven were constructed during the time of the Knights).

The Gate of d'Amboise (also called Protomastoras by the Greeks) was built in

The Gate of d'Amboise, dating from 1512.

1512 by Grand Master Emery d'Amboise (1505-1512). The bridge in front of it was once a drawbridge that continued to be raised every night up to the time of the Italian occupation. In Orfeos Street, lined with plane-trees, shops and little coffee-houses, anonymous but talented artists will paint your portrait! A little further on is the Gate of St. Anthony (Agios Antonios). Artillery Gate (Kanonion) is connected to a movable bridge leading to the road encircling the walls. In Kleovoulos Square stands the restored Gothic open loggia of St. John which ran from the Palace across to the magnificent three-aisled Church of St. John of the Collachium (Fig. II, 3), the order's patron. It was built in the first half of the 14th century in the Gothic style; the Grand Masters were buried here. During the Turkish occupation it was converted into a mosque, as were many of the town's churches. It was levelled on November 6, 1856 in an explosion caused when lightning struck its bell-tower and ignited a forgotten munitions cache.

There was a legend that in the basement of the Castle or under the bell-tower a large quantity of gunpowder was stored, hidden there in 1522 by d'Amaral to get revenge on Grand Master de l'Isle-Adam. Successive pashas never checked out the rumour, and this resulted in the destruction of approximately 250 buildings in the Street of the Knights and 800-1000 deaths. A Swedish doctor, John Hedenborg, estimated that there were 300 tons of gunpowder!

All that remains of the Church today is a segment of a wall; a Turkish school (Fig. II, 4) was built on the site. There was also a prison for aristocratic criminals here, until some point in the Italian occupation.

Judging from the arms of Grand Master Helion de Villeneuve (1319-46) on the left side of its entrance, restoration and repair works must have begun on the Palace of the Grand Masters (Fig. II, 1) immediately after the arrival of the Knights, so that it could be used as a residence for the Grand Masters in times or peace or a place of refuge in times of siege. There is evidence to support the theory that it was built on the spot – at the highest point in the medieval town – where the celebrated sanctuary of the god Helios originally stood, later the site of a 7th-century Byzantine fortress. Building materials from here were probably used to repair the Palace. Today it is certain that a section of the cellars, ground floor and the south side of the Palace are the remains of the Byzantine building.

On the layout and appearance of the Palace during the time of the Knights, scanty information is provided by the historian J. Bosio, who wrote the history of the Knights, by Guillaume Caoursin, who described the siege of 1480, by accounts of travellers and by the few remaining ruins. In the inner courtyard (50 X 40 m) there were vaulted storerooms for animal fodder and military supplies, as well as underground silos for storing grain. Edouard Biliotti has estimated that there was underground space under the Palace on three levels. The archaeologist Albert Berg believed that these basements were used as storerooms and places of refuge for women and children in times of danger, as prisons for captive Muslims, and as a treasure house.

The layout of the Palace's rooms around the central courtyard, with storerooms on the ground floor and living quarters on the upper floor, is indicative of the Byzantine influences it received. On the ground floor the military garrison was lodged (official chambers, living quarters and toilets). It is more difficult to describe the upper story because, together with part of the ground floor, it collapsed in the 1856 explosion. The existence of a meeting hall and Chapel of St. Catherine and Mary Magdalen have been mentioned. (It is said

Only a few ruins remain today of the Church of St. John of the Collachium. A Turkish school was built on its site.

that bones from the hand of St. Catherine and a thorn from Christ's crown of thorns that bloomed every year on Good Friday were once kept here!) In general, however, misuse of the building by the Turks had already caused its partial collapse even before the earthquakes and the explosion.

Although the Italians made an important contribution and the results of their in-

The Italians may not have respected the history of the Palace of the Grand Master during their restoration work, but there is no doubt that they transformed it into an impressive building.

View of the Palace from the south, where its main gate stands, in exactly the same place it occupied in the time of the Knights

tervention on the Palace are impressive, their work cannot be considered mere restorations. The present Gothic building of porous stone is an almost complete reconstruction, begun in 1933, when Lago was still governor. Planning and supervision of the work were undertaken by the Italian architect Vittorio Mesturino. Work was completed in 1939, at a final cost of 170,000,000 pre-war drachmas! The grandiose three-story building was made much larger than its predecessor (75X80 m); it contains 158 rooms. Its exterior was restored to its former appearance – despite minimal additions and alterations – but its austere character was altered by the provocatively luxurious interior decoration, an expression of the megalomania of its builders, along with efforts to impose

Porcelain plaque, built into the wall of the inner courtyard, in the form of an open book

fascist ideology. It was intended as a residence for de Vecchi and a summer residence for King Vittorio Emmanuele III and Mussolini, but the latter never made it to Rhodes. The Italian administration also had its offices here. Underground chambers were used for torturing and imprisoning resistance fighters. During the German occupation, it served the same purposes. The last occupying force, the British, stole valuables from the Palace.

At the entrance to the Palace of the Knights (opening hours 8:30 am-3:00 pm daily except Mondays), built into the wall to the left of the outer entrance is a porcelain plaque in the form of an open book. Its left-hand page has a Latin text signed by J. Fontanus, and on the right-hand page there is a Greek translation of the Latin. It recounts the tragic story of a beautiful Greek lady, whose husband, an English warrior who was leader of the Order of the Knights, expired in the siege of 1522 before her eyes. The unhappy mother embraced and kissed her children for the last time, threw them in the fire, and, donning her husband's bloody uniform, fought valiantly in the first ranks and killed many Turks before she was killed herself.

The main gate of the Palace, between two horseshoe-shaped towers, is one of the surviving fragments of the original building. On the north side of the inner courtyard 1st- and 2nd-century statues stand on bases; they were brought here

The inner courtyard was adorned with 2nd- and 1st-century BC statues from Kos.

A Renaissance chapel on the ground floor of the Palace

from the Roman Odeum on the island of Kos. The heads obviously do not belong to these statues, but were added when the Palace was rebuilt. The courtyard is used for concerts and recitals.

Today a portion of the Palace is open to the public. On the ground floor is its Renaissance chapel, which houses a bronze copy of a statue of St. Nicholas, by the famous Florentine sculptor Donatello (1386-1466). There is also an important collection of objects from the time of the Knights, including maps, important icons, etc.

On the ground floor and the underground levels of the Palace there has been a permanent exhibition since 1993 to commemorate the 2400th anniversary of the founding of the city. A wealth of archaeological material is on display, most of which has come to light in excavations carried out on the island during the last 45 years (opening hours 8:30 am-14:30 pm

The grand staircase of the Palace

daily except Mondays).

The first floor of the Palace is a small museum, whose exhibits are limited to what has remained of its sumptuous decorations and fittings. The wooden ceilings are held up by Roman columns and the alabaster windows offer a magical view of the gardens, the town and the sea. The floors are of coloured marble or Hellenistic, late Roman and early Christian mosaics from Kos. Also worth seeing is the throne

The first floor of the Palace is a small museum whose exhibits are restricted to what has remained of its luxurious furnishings and equipment.

The mosaic of the nine Muses dating from the first century AD, and a Roman mosaic depicting a monster carrying a nymph

room, with the mosaic of the nine Muses dating from the 1st century AD. Outstanding among the other mosaic floors are the Roman mosaic depicting a seahorse carrying a nymph, the delicately executed mosaic of a winged fisherman, the mosaic of the giant Polybotes and Poseidon, and the mosaic of a Medusa's head. On a big marble Hellenistic altar from Ialisus with bas-

Dockyard Gate at the NW end of the harbour

reliefs of Dionysus and the Maenads, a 1st-century BC marble sepulchral trophy which once adorned the grave of a general has been placed. Without doubt the loveliest piece in the Palace is the plaster cast of the Laocoön group, a "gift" of the Vatican Museum, which houses the original. The furniture consists of pieces of various styles and epochs (15th-19th centuries), including some rare Renaissance pieces from Italian churches. The governor's office contains original 16th-century furniture. In other rooms there are large fireplaces, chandeliers, candelabra, wooden chests, tablecloths with Rhodian embroidery, a huge Chinese vase, lovely screens covered with embroidery, etc. There are also music rooms, ballrooms and a dining room with a marble table and wooden pews with carved backs.

In the garden of the Palace (garden of the deer), planted with tropical flowers, are the sarcophagi of a few Grand Masters, and the bronze she-wolf suckling Romulus and Remus (symbol of ancient Rome), which the Italians had set up opposite the one deer statue to grace the moles at the entrance to Mandraki harbour. The Palace provides a spectacular sight when it and the walls are lit up at night.

From Mandraki, which was occupied during the rule of the Knights by minor artisan shipbuilders, you will pass through **Liberty Gate** (Eleftherias), which was not part of the original plan, but was opened up by the Italians to facilitate traffic in 1924. You emerge into Simi Square. A little to the north is the **Gate of St. Paul** (Agiou Pavlou), through which the tower of the same name communicated with the square tower of Naillac which stood on the end of the mole. You will come out onto the road along the waterfront in the commercial harbour through **Dockyard Gate** (Nafstathmou or Tarsana), built on the NW end of the harbour to provide communication between the dockyard and the harbour (Emborio).

We do not hesitate to recommend a visit to the Municipal Picture-Gallery (Fig. II, 70) in Simis Square, housed on the upper story of a restored medieval building. It was created by Andreas Ioannou, Prefect of the Dodecanese (1916-1972), and contains works by famous 20th-century Greek painters, engravers and sculptors, such as Parthenis, Gounaropoulos, Tsarouhis, Hatzikiriakos-Gikas, Moralis, Theofilos, Tombros, Apartis, Karahalios, etc. (opening hours 8:00 am-14:30 pm daily, except Mondays). The oldest structure in this square is the ruined temple (Fig. II, 5) of Aphrodite (?), dating from the 3rd century BC.

Behind the temple is Argirokastrou Square. The Italians adorned this square with an early Christian baptismal font they brought from the Church of Agia Irini of Arnitha and converted into a fountain. This font was made in the 5th-6th century AD of firestone. (The early Christians baptised adults, not babies!) Behind it stands a

"Byzantine Landscape" by Fotis Kontoglou, tempera on wood (Rhodes Municipal Gallery)

building (Fig. II, 6) built by Grand Master Roger de Pins (1355-1365), whose coat of arms can be seen on its façade. This building probably served as the first hospital of the Knights. Later it was used as an arsenal for the Knights and the Turks (hence the former name of Argirokastrou Square, Piazza dell'Armeria). Today it houses the offices and library of the Insti-

The ruins of the 3rd-century BC temple of Aphrodite (?). In the background the mansion of Hassan Bey can be seen on the left, and the Inn of the Tongue of Auvergne on the right.

The inside of the lid of a chest, showing a love story in three stages (Rhodes Museum of Traditional Decorative Arts)

tute of Archaeology of the Dodecanese (which was founded and run from 1947 to 1959 by the unforgettable archaeologist I. Kondis). Further on in the same building, in the Museum of Traditional Decorative Arts (Fig. II, 7), you will see representative examples of the popular culture of the Dodecanese. It includes exhibits covering the years from 1523 to 1912, among them local costumes, embroidery and woven materials, reconstructions of rooms, objects of glass, clay and faience (with raised enamel decoration) (opening hours 8:30 am-15:00 pm, except Mondays). The stone balls at the corner of the building date from the siege of 1522.

Stone balls (of porous stone or local grey marble) may be found stacked in several places in the Old Town. They were used in the catapults during Demetrius' siege; the lightest weigh 5 minas (2.18 kg) and the heaviest 600 minas (261.6 kg.).

On the opposite side of the square, near the city wall, stands the mansion of Hassan Bey (Fig. II, 9), and to the right the Inn of the Tongue of Auvergne (Fig. II, 8), completed in 1507.

Entering the Old Town through the small **Arnaldo Gate**, you come to Museum Square; on your left is the Inn of the Tongue of England (Fig. II, 2), which was destroyed in 1850 and rebuilt in 1919 by

Argirokastrou Square, with the early Christian baptismal font from the Church of Agia Irini in Arnitha. Behind it stands the building from the time of the Knights which houses the office and library of the Archaeological Institute of the Dodecanese. On the left the entrance to the Rhodes Museum of Traditional Decorative Arts can be seen.

Colonel Sir Vivian Gabriel. The British completed it with repairs in 1949.

To your right is the Guy de Melay house (Fig. II, 11), and next to it the Church of St. Mary of the Castle (= Panagia tou Kastrou, the Knights' Catholic Cathedral, Fig. II, 12). It is known to have been in existence in the 13th century, and may have been the seat of the Orthodox Metropolitan from late in the 11th century. Its Byzantine architecture was in part altered to Gothic by the Knights, when its partially completed dome collapsed, possibly in an earthquake. During the Turkish occupation it was converted into a mosque (cami) called Enderoum or Kandouri, but nothing is left to remind us of this phase in its history. It is now a Byzantine museum, with an important collection of icons and frescos from all over Rhodes.

The most important building on the Square is the Hospital of the Knights (Fig. II, 13). Construction work was begun on it in 1440 under Grand Master Jean de Las-

In small rooms under the building's two-story colonnade, finds from the whole island are exhibited by type.

tic (1437-1454), using funds collected by his predecessor, Grand Master Antoine Fluvian (1421-1437). Fluvian himself gave 10,000 florins, according to the inscription recording its founding under the bas-relief in the entrance. It was completed under d'Aubusson (1485). The edifice, 55 m long and 19 m high, was built of porous stone over the ruins of a Roman structure; its architecture is expressive of the Renais-

The Church of St. Mary of the Castle and its inner courtyard

The main entrance to the Hospital of the Knights, which since 1916 has housed the Archaeological Museum of Rhodes

On the building's ground floor is stone catapult shot. In the two-story colonnade and in the museum garden, be sure to see the various architectural members, altars, inscriptions, and sepulchral monuments, spanning the centuries from prehistoric through early Christian times. There are also a few exhibits from other islands in the Dodecanese. The museum's largest room is the Infirmary Ward (51 m long, 12 m wide and 7.5 m high), capable of holding 32 beds. The hall's arches support a ceiling of cypress-wood. Apart from the sick, the Hospital also welcomed pilgrims and the poor. Coats of arms and bas-relief plaques from Crusader times found in the cemeteries of St. John and Panagia tou Kastrou are on display here.

We leave the Museum and climb the Odos Ippoton (Street of the Knights), un-

The little Aphrodite of Rhodes, a late Hellenic reworking of a famous devotional statue of the 3rd century BC

sance outlook inherent in the Gothic style. It was damaged in the siege of 1480 and the earthquake of 1481. Under the Turks, it served as a barracks. In 1914-1916 important repairs were effected by the Italian Ephor of Antiquities responsible for excavations and restorations, Amedeo Maiuri, and it was converted into a museum (opening hours 8:30 am-14:30 pm daily, except Mondays).

Over the entrance to the Hospital, the three windows of the chapel of St. Nicholas, patron Saint of the Knights, can be seen. The door of cypress wood was a gift from Sultan Mahmout to Louis-Philippe (it is now at Versailles). In the main porticoed courtyard of the museum, you will see a marble Hellenistic lion holding the head of a bull between his front paws; in front of him is an early Christian mosaic from Arkassa on the island of Karpathos.

der the impression that we have travelled far back in time. The island's handsomest, stone-paved thoroughfare, 200 m long, is a virtual museum piece, preserved down through the centuries in the same place as the ancient city's "Plateia Odos" (Broad Street), of 408 BC. During the rule of the Knights, a rainwater conduit was added. The Inns of most of the Tongues stood in this street.

The houses and inns of the Knights were all built on the same pattern; they date from the 14th-15th century, and can be divided into two periods of building activity. Up to 1480 Byzantine elements used by local artists predominated, whereas after the devastation caused by the siege of 1480 and the earthquake of 1481 Western European artists introduced elements of the Gothic style, with slight variations on similar buildings in the papal courts of Italy, Spain and Avignon in Provence. They are massive, with impressive flat outer walls, unadorned except for some bas-relief ornamentation on their façades; windows and doors are few. As a rule, they are two-story, flat-roofed structures. On the ground floor and lining the inner courtyard are great storerooms. Living quarters are on the upper story. Towards the end of the first period, a few Renaissance motifs relieved the austerity of the Gothic monastic style. After the devastation caused by the sieges of 1480 and 1552 and by repeated severe earthquakes, almost all the buildings in the street were carefully restored, so as to retain their original appearance.

The second building on your right is the Inn of the Tongue of Italy (Fig. II, 14), built in 1519 under Grand Master Fabrizio del Carretto. Next to it is an unnamed house, bearing the arms of Grand Masters d'Amboise and de l'Isle-Adam on its façade.

The next Inn was that of the Tongue of France (Fig. II, 17). Built between 1492 and 1512 by Grand Masters d'Aubusson and d'Amboise, it is the most harmonious and most richly decorated building in the

In the patients' ward is this ancient sarcophagus, used as a tomb for Grand Master Pierre de Corneillan (1353-1355). The lid is more recent.

street; its façade is 25 m wide. The Turks altered its appearance, but in 1912 the French ambassador to the Porte bought it, and in 1932 repairs were begun on it. Restoration work continued after 1940, and today it is the property of the French state. The building (Fig. II, 15) opposite, with the arched semi-circular lintel and the lovely garden, bears the arms of Diomede de Villaragut.

The northern portal of the Hospital of the Knights

Above: *At the intersection of Ippoton and Lahitos Streets stands the Palace of Villaragut.*
Below: *The extensive façade of the elegant Inn of the Tongue of France*

The 14th-century Church of the Holy Trinity

Also on your right, a narrow street leads to the small single-aisled Church of Agios Dimitrios (Fig. II, 20), built in 1499 by Admiral Ludovico Piossasco on the foundations of a celebrated temple of Dionysus. To your left, in Lahitos Street, stands the Costanzo Operti house (Fig. II, 16).

Returning to the Street of the Knights, on your right you will see an elegant corner house (Fig. II, 18) – perhaps an adjunct of the Inn of France – built in 1510, with a rectangular window-case on the outer door (during the Turkish occupation it was known as the Palace of Zizim or Zem). The small 14th-century church dedicated to the Holy Trinity also belongs to the Inn of the Tongue of France; when it was converted into a mosque it was given the name Han-Zante. On its façade are the arms of Grand Master Raymond Berenger (1365-1374). In a niche is a stone statue of the Virgin and Child. The church's French sacristan lived next door in the two-story building (cappellania, Fig. II, 20) before the arch. In the street on the right (Pissandrou St.) is the house of Nicolas de Montmirel (Fig. II, 23).

Just past the arch we see the Inn of the Tongue of Provence (Fig. II, 25), built in 1518, notable for its elegant door. Just op-

Opposite Page: *Traces of the splendour of its glorious past are what make Rhodes unique. The Street of the Knights today, and in a lithograph made by Rottiers in 1828.*

The Inn of the Tongue of Spain

Above: The house (cappellania) where the French sacristan of the Church of the Holy Trinity lived
Below: The Inn of the Tongue of Provence, dating from 1518, with its elegant door

posite stands the Inn of the Tongue of Spain (Aragon and Castile, Fig. II, 24), separated from Ipparhou Street by the same arch: the room above it belongs to this Tongue. It was built in stages between 1421 and 1512 by Grand Masters Fluvian and d'Amboise.

For a change of atmosphere, start out from the harbour, on which hordes of tourists converge every day. **Marine Gate** (Thalassini; called Porta Marina by the Knights) was built in 1478 by Grand Master d'Aubusson, and bears his coat of arms. It is regarded as being the handsomest of all the gates, with its lofty, almost semi-circular towers and bas-relief of the Virgin flanked by St. Peter and John the Baptist. Between this and Arnaldo Gate stands a Byzantine tower with a medieval chapel (Fig. II, 71).

Our journey back in time continues in the streets and squares of the Old Town. In Ippokratous Square, along with a fountain, is the Castellania (penal court, Fig. II, 28), dating from 1507, one of the few structures built in the late Gothic style known as "flamboyant". This was the Knights' commercial court and centre for commercial and financial transactions (Basilica Mercatorum); it, too, bears the arms of Amboise. It was repaired by the Italians, after the ground floor was used for a time as a fish market and the upper floor, with its painted wooden ceiling, as a museum. Today it houses the Folklore Archives and the Municipal Library. Exhibitions are held in its courtyard.

In Pithagora Street, which starts from Ippokratous Square, is the Mosque of Ibrahim Pasha (Fig. II, 30), built in 1531. It is the city's oldest, but includes more recent additions. It is said that many infidels were hanged from the branches of its venerable plane-tree. At the intersection of Platonos and Apellou Streets, a fragment of the wall of 408 BC remains, along with a square tower, its stairs, and a section of the Byzantine wall (Fig. II, 29).

In Thoukididou Street, which is a continuation of Platonos Street, the large ruined inscribed cruciform Church of the Archangel Michael (Fig. II, 31), dating from the 14th century (Demerli Cami), was built to replace the Orthodox Metropolis, when the Knights converted the Panagia tou Kastrou into a Catholic cathedral. It was bombed during World War II; today all that

The handsome Marine Gate

remain are the central apse of the sanctuary and some frescos. In Athinas Square, near the Church of Agios Spiridon (Kavakli Masjid, Fig. II, 32), a three-aisled domed basilica built over the ruins of an early Christian church, a section of a three-aisled early Christian basilica can be seen in a fenced-off area.

You can experience the atmosphere of the bazaar in Sokratous Street, which is even today the nerve-centre of the me-

The Castellania, built in 1507, in Ippokratous square, is one of the few buildings built in the late Gothic style.

The ruined Church of the Archangel Michael, dating from the 14th century

The Muslim library of Ahmet Havuz, built in 1793

dieval town. In the open-air shops and picturesque coffee-shops everything seems to go on at the same leisurely pace. No one leaves the island without an umbrella or a Rhodian plate, rug or piece of embroidery. At the beginning of the street is Sintrivan Mosque (Fig. II, 26), and in the small square a section of the Byzantine wall and

The Mosque of Ibrahim Pasha, which dates from 1531

ruins of Turkish baths (Fig. II, 27). In the middle of the street stands the 18th-century Mosque of Aga (Fig. II, 33), and at its end the striking Mosque of Suleiman (Fig. II, 34), built in the 16th century on the site of the Church of Agii Apostoli. It is said that it collapsed and was rebuilt using antique materials in 1808. An arch from a 16th-century Renaissance tomb was used as a door frame. (Its elegant minaret has recently been torn down, along with a few others, because it was in danger of falling; it may be rebuilt.) Opposite the mosque, on your right, is the Muslim Library of Ahmet Havuz (Fig. II, 35), founded by a Rhodian Aga in 1793. Among the manuscripts in the Arabian, Persian and Turkish styles in its collection are the chronicle of the occupation of Rhodes by the Turks, and an illustrated Qur'an dating from 1540. In Ippodamou Street stands the Muslim poorhouse (Imaret). Its furnace incorporates the entire vault of the Gothic Church of Agii Apostoli!

To the left of the Mosque of Suleiman, at the intersection of Orfeos and Theofiliskou Streets, stands the Clock Tower, or Guardia Tower, which replaced the 19th-century tower that formed part of the Byzantine enceinte. In Theofiliskou Street, part of the forewall and wall-towers from Byzantine and Crusader times have been discovered. The wall continues into Agissandrou Street, in the middle of which an early Christian basilica was found, which

Above: *Picturesque corners in the medieval town*
Below: *Sindrivan Mosque and the Mosque of Suleiman, one at the beginning and the other at the end of Sokratous Street*

The conventual church of the Monastery of Agios Georgios

had been replaced later by a small cruciform church.

In Apollonion Street, which is a continuation of Sokratous Street – there is a church of interest from an architectural standpoint. It is a three-aisled basilica (Fig. II, 39) with four conchae, believed originally to have been the conventual church of a 14th-15th century Byzantine monastery, possibly dedicated to Agios Georgios. The additions made in the 15th century by the Franciscans have given it a Gothic character. In 1522 it was converted into a Turkish school of theology and was renamed Kurmale Madresah (= "College of the Date-Palm").

The **Gate of St. George** (Agiou Georgiou), built in 1421/31, was walled up and converted into a tower at the beginning of the 16th century. Between this tower and the Gate of St. Athan (Agios Athanassios), the round tower of Spain was built in 1489. A short distance to the north, in Ierokleous Street, stands the small church of Agios Markos (Sadri-Djelebi Masjid, Fig. II, 40).

In 1441 the tower of St. Mary was built, for better protection of the **Gate of St. Athan**. This gate was closed up, according to the Turkish legend, in 1531 by Suleiman himself, to keep anyone else from entering and taking the city; it remained closed until 1922. Through this gate, the visitor will enter the Turkish quarter, containing a number of small churches which have been

The Clock or Guardia Tower

The Gate of St. John or Koskinou

converted into mosques. To the left of the gate stands the single-aisled basilica of St. Athan (in Turkish, Bab-u-Mestud Masjid = Mosque of the built-up gate, Fig. II, 41).

In Andronikou Street is the Church of St. Nicholas or St. Bernard (Abdul Djelel Masjid, Fig. II, 42), either an Orthodox or Catholic three-aisled basilica with many Gothic elements, which was damaged during World War II. In the same street is the Old Town's Folkloric Dance Theatre, where Nelly Dimoglou's Greek dance troupe perform folk dances. In 1765, to the north, in Arionos Square, the Mosque of Sultan Mustapha (Fig. II, 43), with a fountain, and the baths of Mustapha (Fig. II, 44) were built, using marble from ancient buildings.

In Ergiou Street is the Church of Agios Artemios (Sikidi Masjid, Fig. II, 45), and in Menekleous Street, the three-aisled basilica of Agios Konstantinos or Kadi Masjid (Fig. II, 26), with late 14th-century frescos. In the opposite direction, in Ippodamou Street, stands the three-aisled basilica of Agia Paraskevi or Takkeci Masjid (Fig. II, 47), dating from the 15th century, and in Timokreontos Street the Mosque of Hamza Bey (Fig. II, 48).

Both the well-built **Gate of St. John or Koskinou** (Red Gate), dating from 1457, and its towers bear notable escutcheons of Grand Masters, along with a partially destroyed marble bas-relief of St. John. The inside of the gate dates from an older period of fortification. Next to the walls stands the Church of St. John the Baptist, a single-aisled basilica (Kizil Kapu Masjid, Fig. II, 49).

There is a church (Fig. II, 72) of unknown name in Pithagora Street. At the intersection of Pithagora and Omirou Streets stands a medieval windmill (Fig. II, 50). The following single-aisled basilicas can be found in Omirou Street: Agii Theodori (Fig. II, 51), a church from the time of the Knights, converted into the Hundai Masjid; Agia Kiriaki (Boruzan Masjid, Fig. II, 52);

The Mosque of Sultan Mustapha, built in 1765, with fountain, and the baths of Mustapha

61

Above: *The 15th-century Church of Agia Paraskevi*
Below: *The "Serai", a privately-owned house with a room above the arch in Pithagora Street*

The Mosque of Hamza Bey, as seen from the outer road encircling the walls

and, parallel to it, the Church of the Archangel Michael (Alemnaki Masjid = Mosque of the standard-bearer, Fig. II, 53); Turkish tradition has it that it was founded by Suleiman's standard-bearer.)

And of course not to be missed in Dorieos Square, with its fountain, is the magnificent mosque of Redjeb Pasha (Fig. II, 54), built in 1588 with architectural members from churches from Byzantine

St. John the Baptist

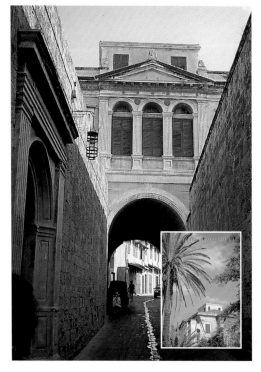

Agia Kiriaki

The Archangel Michael

and Crusader times. Only a few of the porcelain ceramics that once graced its exterior have survived. In the same square is the three-aisled basilica of Agios Fanourios (Fig. II, 55), dating from 1309 built in the shape of an irregular cross, it has a dome and important 13th-15th-century frescos (Turkish name Peial-el-din Masjid).

In the opposite direction, in Dimosthenous Street, is the Church of Agia Marina (Fig. II, 56). The Orthodox Church of

The Mosque of Redjeb Pasha, built in 1588, and its fountain

Agia Marina

Agia Triada (Fig. II, 57), in P. Rhodiou Square, built in the mid-15th century, was

The mid-15th-century Church of Agia Triada

The basilica of Agios Fanourios, dating from 1309

converted into a mosque, the Dolapli Masjid, and the Church of Agia Ekaterini (Fig. II, 58), a three-aisled basilica in Perikleous Street, housing 14th-century frescos, was converted into the Ik Mihrab (= first prayer niche, because it is said that it was here that Suleiman prayed for the first time after entering the city).

Near **Akandia Gate**, one of the older

gates, closed early in the 16th century, the formidable bastion of Italy or del Caretto was built. In the medieval moat, the Open Theatre (Fig. II, 59) holds concerts, performs plays and organises dance productions every summer.

Behind the **Gate of St. Catherine** (Agia Ekaterini), in Pissidorou Square, are the ruins of the Gothic Churches of the Panagia tis Nikis (Our Lady of Victory, Fig. II, 60) and Agios Panteleimon (Fig. II, 61), built to commemorate the defeat of the Turks in the siege of 1480. In front of them, there is a fenced-off portion of the ancient wall (Fig. II, 62). Next to it stands the hospital/ inn of St. Catherine (Fig. II, 63), founded by the Italian Knight Fra Domenica d'Alemagna in 1392. It was repaired in 1516, so that Italian gentlefolk passing through the island could be accommodated or cared for. A Church (Fig. II, 64) in Thisseos Street may have been that of St. Catherine.

In front of **St. Mary's (Panagia) Gate** are the ruins of a small chapel and of the

The Church of Agios Pandeleimon, built in 1480

large Gothic Church of Panagia tis Choras (Our Lady of the City, Fig. II, 65), also known as the Cut Virgin, because part of

The great Gothic Church of Our Lady of the City, or the Cut Virgin

The new Synagogue

the front of the church was torn down to make way for Alhadef Street. Opposite stands the Giovanni Manelli house (Fig. II, 66). The Square of the Evreon Martiron (Jewish Martyrs), the beginning of the once bustling Jewish quarter, is graced by a fountain with bronze seahorses. Just in front of it stands the erroneously named "Palace of the Admiralty" (Fig. II, 67). The inscriptions tell us that this was really the 15th-century archbishop's residence, which served at different times as living quarters for the island's Orthodox or Catholic Archbishop.

In Vizantiou Street is a Catalan house (Fig. II, 69). The Jewish Synagogue (Fig. II, 68) was destroyed in 1480 and rebuilt in Dossiadou Street, with the help of the Knights, after the Jews came to their assistance in the 1480 siege. In Aristotelous Street, you will see many houses with Turkish wooden lattice-work and enclosed wooden balconies.

The Square of the Jewish Martyrs and the fountain with the bronze seahorses. To its left stands the erroneously named "Palace of the Admiralty".

Showcase of Lindos dishes, a gift of I.N. Kazoulis to the Rhodes Museum of Traditional Decorative Arts

Folklore –
The Arts in Modern Times

An important place in the wealth of island folk pottery is occupied by the elaborate Lindos dishes. As was the case with Byzantine art, particular importance was placed on decoration and the high quality of the materials used. Despite the external influences exerted on the artisans (they were significantly influenced both by Muslim and by Persian genius), they produced purely Rhodian creations.

It is said that it was during the time of the Knights, under Grand Master Villeneuve, that the manufacture of Lindos' pottery and ceramic wares was organised, when the Knights' fleet captured the Persian ship "La Carague", Among its passengers were some Persian potters, who were forcibly settled in Lindos in order to teach their art to the locals. The island's first ceramic workshop used simple, primitive methods and materials (fine pink sand from the seashore; later pulverised coral) to manufacture household ware and decorative tiles for houses and churches. The Lindians' art quickly surpassed that of their teachers, and they started up an export trade, mainly in dishes. Manufacture and export of the ware continued during the Turkish occupation.

The most common dishes were round, between 10 and 40 cm in diameter, some in plain colours, usually blue or green, and others multicoloured, again usually blue or green, but sometimes violet, black or bright red. Later more expensive gilded dishes were produced, but they were not as durable. The most common designs included flowers, animals and ships. In addition to the collection of decorative ware in Rhodes, Lindian dishes also grace the Benaki Museum in Athens and the Cluny Museum in Paris.

Despite its economic decline in early

Embroidered silk bedroom screen (Rhodes Museum of Traditional Decorative Arts)

Byzantine times, Rhodes did not fall into stagnation. Its building materials workshops continued to produce white "vissali" (= bricks made out of a mixture of shredded ropes, powdered pumice, flour and other materials; five Rhodian bricks weighed the same as one ordinary brick.) That was the reason why when the Byzantine Emperor Justinian rebuilt St. Sophia in 532 – as the Byzantine chronicler G. Codinos informs us – he obtained a large quantity of vissali from Rhodes (Archangelos or Lindos) for the dome. During the rule of the Emperor Justin (562) the dome was again damaged, and bricks to repair it were again shipped in from Rhodes.

Local weaving flourished already in antiquity, according to Plutarch. Alexander the Great, in the historic Battle of Gaugamela in 331 BC, wore a cape woven and embroidered by Rhodian women. The weavers were called "alefantoudes" or "lefantaries", the loom "vou(v)a", and the embroiderers "ploumistres". Due to Rhodes' sunny clime, the embroidery gracing

homes and costumes had bright, cheerful colours and themes taken from the Byzantine tradition.

In Byzantine times, in addition to sheets and pillowcases, "sperveria" and "mahramades" were embroidered. Sperveria were a type of woven screen, embroidered with locally-produced silk thread, used to enclose the bridal bed. The main colours were various shades of delicate red and green. According to the noted folklorist Athina Tarsouli, such a screen weighed around 20 kilograms (44 lbs.). The "mahramades" were hand-woven lengths of fabric embroidered in gold, used to decorate the large candles at a wedding, and later to adorn the sitting-room. The woven textiles and embroideries were kept in carved wooden chests. Such priceless products of folk tradition, of great artistic merit, survive in good condition in the Rhodes Museum of Traditional Decorative Arts, in the Benaki Museum in Athens, and naturally in some traditional Rhodian sitting-rooms in private collections. The city of Rhodes boasts a rich tradition in weaving, as do the villages of Embona, Soroni, Afandou, Koskinou, Lindos, Archangelos, Genadi and Agios Issidoros.

The oldest musical instruments in the Dodecanese are the lira and the tsambouna. The former is analogous to the Byzantine lyre, which passed from Byzantium to the West during the Middle Ages and evolved into the violin. The latter has two pipes: one has five holes and plays six notes, and the other is of the same length, but only has one hole and plays two notes. Such musical instruments are used to accompany religious songs and carols, as well as lullabies, songs of lamentation, and the traditional folk couplets, or mantinades, as well as to play dance music at the traditional Rhodian weddings, which were once among the island's most important social events.

Most of the dances [Vatani or Gatani, Tzenevetos, Sousta, and Zervodexios (a type of Syrtos)] were performed by both men and women. The leader of such line dances usually clasped the hand of the second person with his right hand, and the right hand of the third person with his left, etc., forming a mesh of arms. In another formation, each dancer stretches out his arms and rests his hands on the opposite shoulder of the person next to him. Only a few dances were performed by one or two people [among them the Tourkikos and the Monahikos (a type of Sousta)].

Present-Day Rhodes

The city of Rhodes, as it expanded after 1522 above the ancient necropolis, more or less covers the same area as the ancient city, not even deviating far from the Hippodamian town plan, as many modern streets are built directly over their ancient counterparts.

On Ammos Point, the island's northern-most tip, is the Hydrobiological Station of Rhodes, which houses an Aquarium of a unique type. The building was built in 1930, probably by the Italian architect Bernabiti, and functioned as a General Biological Institute up to 1935. After the war, it began to be used as a museum of marine organisms. In its impressive tanks you will see interesting species of Mediterranean marine life (opening hours 9:00 am-21:00 pm daily). The island's northern tip is embellished with a series of organised golden sand beaches, studded with colourful umbrellas.

The 8 or 10 medieval windmills scattered along the NW shore seem to be lost in the modern-day luxury of the town's closest extensive cosmopolitan beach. Those who believe they are lucky can put their belief to the test in the casino of the Grand Hôtel Astir Pallas.

Outstanding among the other luxury hotels of the NE coast is the Grand Hotel of the Roses (Albergo Grande delle Rose).

The Rhodes Hydrobiological Station and Aquarium, built in 1930

Organised beaches decked out with colourful umbrellas, to the right and left of the Aquarium

On March 27, 1924, while Lago was governor of the island, its cornerstone was laid, and two years later it was completed. Its total cost was 4,500,000 lire. It had 38 rooms in the basement, 26 on the ground floor, 26 on the mezzanine, 42 on the first and second floors, and 18 on the third. In 1930, the Small Hotel of the Roses was built next to it, with 18 rooms in the basement, 11 on the ground floor, 15 on the first, and 14 on the second and third floors.

In the years between the two World Wars (1918-1939), it was the best hotel in the Mediterranean, and in March 1935, Prime Minister Venizelos stayed there. After Rhodes became part of Greece, it devolved to the Greek state. In 1955 it was taken over by Astir S.A. It was in the sea near this hotel that the 4th century BC statue of Aphrodite (Venus Pudica) was discovered.

On the east side of town you will see

The Grand Hotel of the Roses, where the statue of Aphrodite, somewhat eroded by the seawater, was found

The Rhodes Yachting Club on Ammos Point

The Rhodes Recruiting Office

the old official Muslim cemetery, which was a graveyard for ordinary Knights during Crusader times. The mosque of Suleiman's Admiral Murad Reis with the handsome minaret was originally a church dedicated to Agios Antonios. The circular mausoleum was built here in 1523 to house the still extant sarcophagus of Murad Reis after his heroic death in the siege of 1522. Many other Muslim officials, who died in exile in Rhodes, were buried in the same cemetery, along with other foreign potentates. The lovely Rhodian buildings next to the cemetery house the Rhodes Town-Planning Commission.

Florentano di Fausto, like other Italian architects, used a combination of Gothic, Arabian and Venetian architectural styles when creating the administrative and cultural buildings that line the waterfront. Running along the quay is Eleftherias Street, which leads to Vasileos Georgiou I Square, site of the National Theatre and City Hall. Further on are the Municipal

The old official Muslim cemetery with the Mosque of Murad Reis

City Hall and Rhodes' National Theatre in Vasileos Georgiou I Square

Theatre, where theatrical productions are staged, and the Rhodon cinema/theatre, where traditional holidays are observed and music and dance performances held. A nearby building houses the Government House of the Dodecanese.

Opposite the square is a very important Italian monument, the Prefecture of the Dodecanese building. It was built between 1924-36, when Lago was governor, and served as the Government House. It was here that the Greek flag was first raised in 1947. Floats parade through Eleftherias Street in the framework of the four-day May Flower Festival, which includes a flower show, art exhibits and concerts.

Next to the Prefecture Building is the Archbishop's Palace, and next to it the Cathedral to St. John the Evangelist, with the impressive bell-tower and clock. It was built in 1925 by the Italians, on the model of the Church of St. John of the Collachium, based on engravings made by the Belgian traveller C. Rottiers in 1826 and by

The building housing the office of the Prefect of the Dodecanese

The Archbishop's Palace (left), and the Post Office and Harbour Master's Office (right)

E. Flandin in 1844. (As in most Churches, appropriate dress is required.) The fountain outside is a copy of the great source at Viterbo (a town north of Rome); it dates from the 13th century. At the end of the mole, a column supports one of the two deer that grace the entrance to Mandraki harbour.

Opposite stand the Post Office and next to it the Harbour Master's Office, with handsome bas reliefs, the Courts Building

The Rhodes Courts Building

The Cathedral of St. John the Evangelist, built on the model of the Church of St. John of the Collachium

and the Bank of Greece.

Eleftherias Street embraces Mandraki (taken from the word mandri, meaning sheep-pen, often used to describe small, enclosed ports). The statues of the stag and doe that grace the moles at the harbour entrance are regarded as the symbols of Rhodes; the Italians had replaced one of them with a she-wolf, which the Rhodians

removed in 1947. Small ships sail from here on one-day cruises to Lindos, Simi, Kos and Kalymnos. Flying dolphins serve Tilos and Nissiros twice a week.

On the mole, between Mandraki and the commercial harbour, the sturdy tower of St. Nicholas was built in 1464-67 under Grand Master Zacosta. It cost 10,000 gold crowns, provided by the Duke of Burgundy. (Their arms grace its entrance.) In 1480 d'Aubusson added a polygonal bulwark around the tower's moat. These fortifications played an important part in the sieges of 1480 and 1522. Today the tower is used as a lighthouse. Near it, remnants of the ancient jetty can be seen. On the quay leading to the lighthouse of Agios Nikolaos stand three mills which were mentioned by a traveller as early as 1496. Here, as in the general area of the har-

As your ship approaches the island, the town unfolds before your eyes in all its magnificence and grace. The Palace of the Grand Master, the New Market and the windmills on the mole of Agios Nikolaos, lit up at night
Opposite page: The tower of St. Nicholas, a fortress in itself, at the end of the ancient breakwater of Mandraki, and the deer gracing its entrance

The entrance to the New Market, and a view of its colourful interior

bour, luxury pleasure craft are moored. On the other side of the quay stretches a small beach suitable for swimming.

The Italians' town-planning intervention sapped the strength of the Old Market and gave an impetus to the New Market created outside the city walls. This huge heptagonal, roofed, Turkish-style market became the heart of the modern city. The gardens surrounding it used to be the vast Ottoman cemeteries, abolished under the Italian occupation. The City of Rhodes Philharmonic holds several concerts each summer in the pavilion.

Behind the New Market, "Sound and Light" shows are given in various languages (Greek, English, French, German and Swedish) every evening. The island's history is played out before your eyes like a fairy-tale, in a unique, unforgettable way.

You can make your purchases in Kiprou Square, where some of the town's best stores are to be found. Mingle in among the joyous crowds of tourists and shop for textiles, furs, cosmetics, jewellery and souvenirs of the island.

In Ethnarhou Makariou Street, excavations in 1960 brought to light a cellar containing about a hundred intact amphorae, dating from 227 BC. In Amerikis Street, in the foundation the Zissimatos building, the façade of an ancient house has survived.

The Gate of St. Paul communicated with the square tower of Naillac which stood at the end of the mole until it was demolished in an earthquake in 1863 (it is pictured on many 19th-century engrav-

In the gardens of the Market, vendors offer their tourist wares at outdoor stalls.

The pavilion in Mandraki. Behind it the building housing the Bank of Greece can be seen.

ings). It was built by Grand Master Phillibert de Naillac (1396-1421) on the walled breakwater, and is a superb example of coastal defence. A thick chain was stretched from it across the water to the round Tower of Windmill Mole or of France – whose building was financed by the King of France in the latter part of the 15th century – to protect the commercial harbour. Of the 13 windmills which once stood on this mole, today only three remain. Vessels sail daily from Rhodes' commercial harbour to Marmaris in Turkey, Limassol in Cyprus and Haifa in Israel.

But the medieval town and its harbours are not the only sights to see. A tour of the part of town lying outside the walls will complete the picture of greatness of a civilisation thousands of years old. From the harbour of Akandia, Vironos Street begins; it runs along the outside of the walls through parks will trees and flower-gardens. This is the preferred route of admirers of the walls, walkers and joggers. Along the way you will encounter the Catholic Church of St. Francis outside the Gate of St. Athan (Agiou Athanassiou).

The Gate of St. Paul

Serious athletes, however, will prefer the modern stadium of the local football team, Diagoras, where concerts are held during the summer. Near the stadium an early Christian basilica with mosaic floors was discovered in 1930.

In Anastassias Street, excavations were carried out on a large complex of chamber tombs and foundations of large Hellenistic houses belonging to wealthy townspeople (one such house yielded the impressive mosaics of the Centaur and Bellerophon).

You will continue along Dimokratias

A thick chain linked the Tower of Naillac to the round tower on Windmill Mole.

The modern stadium of Diagoras

The entrance to the neoclassical Rhodian Villa

Street in an equally lush environment, and then climb Papalouka Street. You will be enchanted by the superb Rhodian Villa, where art exhibitions are held. On the ground floor of the building the Rhodes Municipal Library is housed.

The visitor may continue on Papalouka Street and come out of the town on the other side, where the sandy western shore of the island stretches before him, or he may climb up to the acropolis via Voriou Ipirou Street, in which case he will pass some fenced-off temples of nymphs. Alter-natively, he may also take any one of the other streets intersecting with Enoplon Dinameon Street. At the foot of the ancient acropolis, where Himaras and P. Mela Streets meet, another large early Christian basilica has been found, with mosaic floors dating from the 5th century AD; it was probably destroyed in the mid-7th century during the Arab invasion. The street parallel to it, Diagoridon, follows the path of the ancient street that led to the acropolis.

The acropolis of the ancient city crowns the hill of Agios Stefanos, named after a

The impressive island of the sun god and of the Knights will win you over with its natural beauties.

Panoramic view of the town from Voriou Ipirou Street, equally charming by day and by night

Byzantine church that was destroyed by the Turks. It is also known as Monte Smith, after the English Admiral Sir Sydney Smith (1764-1840), who set up watch here to monitor Napoleon's fleet, which was campaigning in Egypt.

The acropolis was discovered in 1916, and excavations were conducted from 1924 to 1929. Today we can see three restored columns supporting a section of architrave, with metopes, cornices, etc. from a temple of Pythian Apollo in a temenos. To the northeast, another building was unearthed, believed to have been a temple of Artemis.

North of the temple of Pythian Apollo, the important temple of Zeus Polieus and Athena Polias came to light: it was a repository for the treaties the ancient Rhodians concluded with other cities. (The epithets Polieus and Polias indicated that these were the patron gods of the city, and their temple was used as an archives for public correspondence, as a treasury, etc.) In 163 BC the Romans set up a statue of colossal proportions (14 m. high) here. To

The sun god Helios never stopped loving his island or bathing it his loveliest colours all day long.

79

At the foot of the hill, the Italians restored the stadium and the theatre.

the west and east of it nymphaea have been discovered.

The Italians made some rather hasty restorations, with little regard for dates or original appearance, to the 201-meter stadium, where only a few ranks of seats in the centre of the sphendone date from the 2nd century BC, and to the theatre, with a capacity of 800, where only two or three seats in the first row and a few steps of the stairs on the left are from the original building. The celebrated gymnasium has also

Neoclassical folk architecture in a house in a marassi

been identified from inscriptions.

The isolated Greek population, who worked inside the walls during the time of Turkish rule, but were forced to live outside them, created populous suburbs south of the castle. Known as marassia (from the Turkish "maras"), each of these suburbs took its name from the Church around which it grew up. The architecture of the houses was quite similar to that of the island's villages. Other influences include medieval architecture and that of nearby islands, as well as neoclassicism later on. The last marassi, Niohori, was built north of the medieval town in the 18th century by wealth Rhodians, consuls and merchants.

Excursions Outside of Town

Karakonero – Rodini

On the way out of the south side of Rhodes town, just before Kallitheas Avenue you will encounter Rhodes' old cemetery, with tombs dating from 1935.

On the left-hand side of Kallitheas Avenue, in the **Karakonero** area, are cemeteries from Classical and Hellenistic times. Outstanding among the area's groups of tombs is a sepulchral sanctuary decorated with figures in bas-relief carved out of the rock, in a representation of a group of Dionysian players. Its exterior decoration must have been completed by lush vegetation and marble grave monuments. On the opposite side of the road are the newer Muslim and Greek cemeteries, as well as the Italian cemetery.

On the way to Asgourou stands an imposing Hellenistic mausoleum of huge dimensions, hollowed out of a small hill of soft rock. Its façade mimics the façade of an arcade or a house; this type of tomb was very common in Rhodes in ancient times. Tree roots have destroyed its sides, and as it was covered with vegetation, we can only assume that it had a pyramidal crown. During the Turkish occupation it was known as "koufon vounin" (= hollow mountain). Foreign travellers erroneously called it the "tomb of the Ptolemies", perhaps confusing it with the monument erected by the Rhodians in the city, or led astray by a coin from the time of the Egyptian kings. It was restored in 1924. Nearby are a number of other groups of tombs, whose dates range from the 3rd century BC up to early Roman times.

Whether you take the inner road, which passes through the ancient graveyards, or return to the main road, you will reach **Rodini Park**, with plenty of greenery. The abundant water running through this valley once supplied the city. Deer and wild goats are among the animals kept here. Excavations on the surrounding rocks have revealed nymphaea. This area, not much changed in appearance since Hellenistic times, is now thought to have had associa-

The imposing mausoleum of the "Ptolemies"

tions with the School of Rhetoric of Aeschines. Exploitation of the natural landscape in a necropolis such as Rodini, despite its rather macabre overtones, allows it to be used as a place for walking and recreation. Its many flowers caused the Turkish conquerors to call Rodini a paradise of hyacinths. Nowadays a wine festival is held here every summer. From this area come a few remnants of a Roman villa containing a mosaic floor which included an emblem portraying some personage, as was common at that time.

A tomb found near the Agia Triada settlement had niches hewn out of the rock and a vaulted roof supported by four fully sculpted Caryatids. Many groups of tombs were discovered on the road to Koskinou.

Idyllic Rodini Park

Excursions in the Island

Rhodes – Ialissos – Valley of the Butterflies – Faliraki – Kallithea

The Bay of Ialissos, just as enchanting by day as it is by night

The northwestern tip of Rhodes, as seen from Philerimo

Rhodes Town is so enchanting and full of interesting things to see that you can easily fall under its spell. But don't make the mistake of spending your whole holiday there. The island's excellent road network makes it easy to venture into its interior, whose wealth of historical and natural points of interest will give you a better overall picture of Rhodes.

Starting from the NW side of town, you can follow the route that takes in almost all the villages of the ancient city-state of Ialysia. First you will encounter **Kritika**, a quarter of town containing the identical small houses of the Turkish refugees who fled here during the war between Turkey and Crete. Below the road stretches the town's second large beach.

On the right side of the road is the Cave of the Dragon, where legend has it that in an epic battle Grand Master Dieudonné de Gozon (1346-1353) killed a dragon (probably a crocodile, judging from the descriptions), which had been terrorising the island's countryside.

From Kritika we travel along **Ixia**, beloved of the smart set. The area is dotted with hotel complexes vying with each other in luxury, along with all types of restaurants and night spots.

Characteristic neo-classical mansions in Ialissos

A different picture is presented by **Ialissos** (from the Phoenician "yelsin" = place of thick vegetation, a pre-Hellenic place-name). Before 1975, the village was called "Trianda" [= village of the andriandas (statue)], from the legend that two old men buried a statue here to keep the Turks from finding it. Or the name may refer to the fact that small farmers bought large parcels of land and divided them into 30 (trianda) parts in order to cultivate them, or to the fact that the area was first settled by 30 refugees.

The 17th-century Church of the Dormition of the Virgin, with its grandiose baroque bell-tower

Although it can accommodate any number of visitors in its 130 hotels and 25,000 rented rooms, Ialissos retains the atmosphere of a Rhodian farming village. The beach here, relatively sheltered from the winds, offers a combination of sand and big white pebbles.

In the town square stands the 17th-century Church of the Dormition of the Virgin, with a finely-carved wooden altar screen dating from 1810 and a somewhat grandiose baroque bell-tower. Nearby is the small chapel of Agios Nikolaos, with superb 15th-century frescos. The plain is dotted with Crusader-era towers and neo-classical mansions. No one visiting the island during the first half of August should miss the "Ialysia" festival, including danoos performed by troupes from all over Greece and concerts by the municipal Philharmonic, in parallel with wine festivals. During the same season, members of the folk dance workshop gives performances dressed in

The area's beach is ideal for water sports.

costumes of their own creation. In summertime, a traditional house, restored on the initiative of the Women's Cultural League of Ialissos, is open to visitors in the town square.

The island's most ancient organised settlement (1550-1400 BC) came to light off the right side of the road leading to Ialissos (Trianda) beach. It was first discovered by the Italians in 1935, but systematic excavations did not begin until May 1978. They revealed traces of a set-

tlement on three levels: one dating from 1550-1500 BC, a second from 1500-1450 BC and a third from 1450-1300 BC. The first, a Minoan settlement of the Late Bronze Age, parallel in time and culture to the major settlements of the Aegean area (Agia Irini on Kea, Filakopi on Milos, Akrotiri on Santorini and Knossos on Crete) was buried under ash when the Santorini volcano erupted around 1500 BC. A second, larger settlement grew up on the site when the wealth brought in by trade and shipping made it possible to replace the old buildings with new, impressive palaces on the Cretan model. It was, however, destroyed in a powerful earthquake. The third settlement quickly sprang up, but ceased to exist after the Achaean invasion.

The houses which have been unearthed had rooms demarcated by wellbuilt walls with bases made of great unhewn stones and mud. They were covered with coloured plaster on the inside, which was usually bright red, but sometimes blue

Figure III: *Plan of Filerimo plateau, based on a topographical drawing by the honourable ephor of antiquities G. Konstantinopoulos*

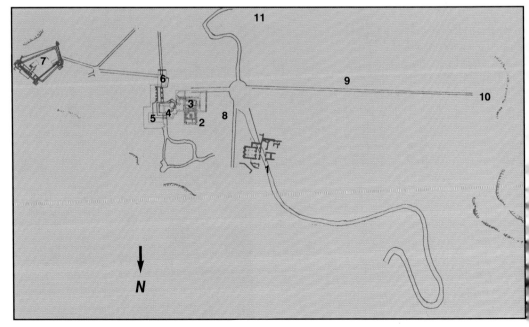

or off-white, and decorated with simple linear designs. Most of the floors were of tamped-down earth, but in some cases they were paved with river pebbles or crushed murex shells. The pottery, earthenware jars, stone tools, small objects of everyday use and clay loom weights found here belong to the settlement's final phase.

In Trojan times, when Rhodes was divided into three parts, ancient Ialysia occupied its northern, more fertile half. Homer mentions that its first settler was Ialysus. The town minted coins on the Phoenician model showing an eagle's head and a winged boar. When the Persians entered the Aegean and mighty Lindus lost her power on the seas, the aristocratic clans of Ialysus continued to amass wealth, as their rural economy was not influenced by the invaders.

Above the village of Ialissos (Trianda), on pine-clad Mt. Filerimo (267 m.), stand Ialysus' monuments, representing the island's whole march through history (opening hours 8:00 am-5:00 pm daily; 8:30 am-3:00 pm Saturday, Sunday and Monday).

The first traces of habitation, in the plain of Ialissos, date from the second millennium (Middle Bronze Age). Judging from the rich offerings found in Mycenean tombs in the surrounding burial grounds, there must have been a settlement or a stronghold here already in Mycenean times. The bellicose Achaeans founded the fortress of Ialysus here: up to the 3rd century BC it was known as "Achaea". Strabo called it "the fortification", and from the Middle Ages to date its name has been "Filerimo".

Phorbas was a settler from mainland Greece. He was the son of a Lapith and the leader of colonies in Helis and Thessaly. The Rhodians invited him to settle on their island, after a prophecy by the Delphic oracle that he would help them get rid of the poisonous snakes that were decimating the inhabitants. He was honoured as a

Flights of steps lead up to the Filerimo's archaeological site.

hero after his death. A more naive version of the same myth tells us that Phorbas' ship sank near Schedia harbour in Ialysus, and the hero and his sister Parthenia enjoyed the warm hospitality of Thamneas. So they settled on the island, and Phorbas asked to be honoured after his death with sacrifices, at which the presence of slaves would be forbidden.

The Rhodian historian Ergeius reports that the Greek Iphiclus conquered the island and drove out the Phoenicians along with their leader Phalanthus from Achaea (Filerimo). The myth goes like this: An oracle had prophesied that the Phoenicians would hold the acropolis until crows turned white and fish swam in wine-bowls! Phalanthus, certain that he would withstand the siege since he held the spring, became complacent. But Iphiclus learned of the secret prophecy, either from a traitor, or, according to a more romantic version, from Dorcia, his opponent's daughter who had fallen in love with him. Having put fish in the wine-jug of a slave of Phalanthus, he waited until he called for his wine to let loose some crows, painted with plaster, along with his men. The Phoenicians, in a panic, began to negotiate. Iphiclus promised to give them ships in which to escape the island, and allowed them to take with them "as much as their bellies would hold." Phalanthus then slaughtered the animals, removed their entrails and

All that remains today of the south aisle of the early Christian church and its baptistery

filled them with valuables. When the trick was noticed, Phalanthus contended that what he had done was permissible. Iphiclus then reminded him that he had promised him ships, but not oars!

That part of the myths that can be said to be a hazy memory of real historical events is substantiated by archaeological finds. First to carry out excavations (1859) was the archaeologist and illicit dealer in antiquities Alfred Biliotti (1836-1871) on behalf of the British Museum; his work was continued later by Italian archaeologists (1935). You can park your car in the square with the oak-tree, and after touring the site relax in its shade and have a cool drink at the refreshment stand. You can then climb the stairs flanked by cypress-trees. On your left-hand side, below the church, lie the foundations of the only ancient building excavated on the mountain, the porous-stone amphiprostyle Doric temple of Ialysian (Polias) Athena (Fig. III, 2), dating from the 3rd/2nd centuries BC; architectural members from it are scattered over the site. Inside the sekos (main temple) the foundations of the inner colonnade and the rectangular base of the cult statue have survived. It is certain that Athena was worshipped in this area at least as far back as the 9th century BC. Important examples of miniature and plastic art dating from the 8th century BC were unearthed in the temple's refuse pit. Terra cotta gorgoneia (=

The restored Crusader church. To the west of it lie the foundations of the Doric temple of Ialysian Athena.

representation of Gorgons' heads used as decorative elements) from the 5th century BC found here testify to the existence of an older, Classical-Age temple.

Materials from the ruined temple were used in the 5th-6th centuries AD to construct the early Christian three-aisled basilica of Filerimo (Fig. III, 3), which occupied most of its site. Of this church, parts of the marble-slabbed floor and the main baptistery, with its font dug out in the shape of a cross and two steps for the person being baptised to descend, are all that remain. Today it is not known just how long this church remained standing. At any rate, a small domed church was built in the northern aisle of the basilica during the 10th century AD.

In the first half of the 14th century, the Knights built the church (Fig. III, 4) seen today; it was slightly altered during restorations by the Italians. Under Grand Master d'Aubusson the two hexagonal chapels and the celebrated bell-tower were added. Today its elongated Gothic windows are much admired. During the German occupation its dome was bombed.

A miraculous 12th-century icon of the Virgin, studded with precious stones and said to have been painted by St. Luke, was kept in this church by the devout; it was taken to the city for greater security and was carried through the town in a procession in times of pestilence and disaster. When they finally abandoned the island, the Knights carried it to Malta, where Napoleon stripped it of its precious ex votos. When the Russian Czar Paul I became Grand Master of the Order in 1799, he took it to Petrograd. After the 1917 Revolution, it was taken to the Yugoslavian palace, whence all trace of it was lost. When the Italians restored the monastery, they placed a copy of the icon in the church.

There are many stories associated with Filerimo monastery. One tells of a noble Rhodian who decided to put an end to his

The inner courtyard of Filerimo's Monastery

life by jumping off the mountain's sheerest cliff. St. Mary appeared before him and rebuked him for what he was about to do. The nobleman decided to build a hermitage on that spot and become a monk. He went to Jerusalem and obtained a miraculous icon of the Virgin for the church of Filerimo. It was not long before the icon became widely known for the miracles it performed, and numbers of the faithful began to climb the mountain to pay homage to it.

The story of two young lovers ends less happily: As they did not have their parents' consent to marry, they met in secret in the sanctuary behind the icon of the Virgin, where they were struck by lightning! According to the story, that is the source of the name Filerimo (= mountain of unhappy love). In reality the mountain was named after a landholder in the area.

An engraving by Rottiers showing the ruined Crusader church of Filerimo during the 19th century

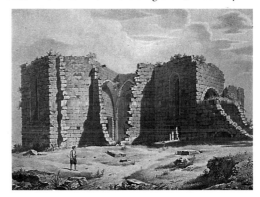

The Byzantine stronghold of Filerimo, which was fortified later by the Knights

It is said that a relic consisting of the arm of St. Philip was kept at the monastery until it was taken to Jerusalem in the 13th century.

On the site of an older monastery, originally used by the Knights and converted by the Turks into a barn, stands the present-day monastery of Filerimo (Fig. III, 5), restored as part of the more general efforts of the Italians to revive the architectural style of the Knights. On the ground floor, lining the colonnaded courtyard with its outdoor pulpit – in accordance with to the Catholic dogma – are the cells of the Franciscan monks, whose walls are graced by mosaics with figures of Saints. On the ground floor of the building next door there are more cells and rooms for common use; on the upper floor was a roofed vaulted arcade leading to the abbot's quarters (Fig. III, 6). An exterior stone staircase leads to its enclosed stone balcony. The courtyard is graced by a stone well.

Behind the monastery, on the SE edge of Filerimo, the Byzantines and the Knights after them built a special stronghold (Fig. III, 7) to fortify the height. This was the most intact fortification complex restored before World War II, during which it was extensively damaged. The walled site contains a large room, which was probably the administration headquarters, and a staircase leading to an upper story with more rooms. On the right and left stand two

Rooms in the Monastery, and next to them the Abbot's quarters

The Way of the Cross, with the imposing cross at the end

Byzantine towers. To the NW a kitchen has been identified. More generally, the stronghold is a combination of Byzantine (large stones or ancient column drums) and medieval buildings (small rectangular stones). It has associations with important historical events. It was here that the Genoese laid siege to General John Cantacuzene's forces in 1248. In 1306 it became the first headquarters of the Knights. In 1522 Suleiman set up his headquarters here, and during the Second World War the Italians installed their artillery on this site.

After returning to the site of the ancient temple, you can walk down to the small single-aisled chapel of Agios Georgios Hostos (Fig. III, 8), coeval with the Byzantine church. Its interior walls are graced with splendid 14th- and 15th-century frescos, in the style of the Knights, with Byzantine influences.

To the left of the square where you left your vehicle are the ruins of the small three-aisled inscribed cruciform domed conventual church of a 10th-century Byzantine monastery (Fig. III, 1).

From the square, a road begins which runs to the westernmost point of the Filerimo plateau. Here the Catholics' Way of the Cross (Fig. III, 9) is lined with stations bearing bronze bas-reliefs of the different stages of Christ's passion. At the end of the road, the 16-meter cross (Fig. III, 10) demolished by the Italians has been rebuilt. Hollow inside, it has a staircase leading to its arms, from which there is a marvellous view.

For the last eight years, the road leading to a well-preserved Doric fountain of porous stone has been closed due a landslide. Despite the fact that its inscription – setting out restrictions and penalties for its misuse – is late Hellenistic, archaeologists have dated the fountain to the 4th century BC. Two conduits brought water down from the mountain, which flowed out of marble lions' heads into a small cistern hollowed out of the rock. The main building

Splendid 14th- and 15th-century frescos in the chapel of Agios Georgios Hostos

89

The Church of Panagia Kremasti

at the fountain, in the shape of an open-ended rectangle, was closed at the front by a Doric colonnade, of which two of the six columns have been restored.

Ialysia, in contrast to the island's other two city-states, had no centralised residential centre, only small villages scattered throughout the plain (11 townships, according to the inscriptions), a fact attested

The small castle of the Knights in Kremasti, inhabited today by a little old lady!

to by the abundant Mycenean, Geometrical, Archaic, Classical and Hellenistic artefacts from the rich graveyards round about (Makra Vounara, Moshou Vounara, Drakidis, Tsambikou, Marmaro, Pavli, etc.). At Makra Vounara, for example, a Mycenean installation of 1450-1200 BC has been excavated, with beehive tombs containing rich grave goods. In this area, Zeus and the Telchinian nymph Imalia and their children were worshipped as deities analogous to the Mylantian gods of Camirus.

A turnoff from the coast road brings us to **Pastida** (from the Latin word for fortress), which offers a few rooms to rent. Back on the main road, you will continue on to **Kremasti**. Its name is said to be a corruption of "Gran Maestri" whose summer residence was in the castle of the village. Or it may be due to the fact that the village seems to hang ("kremasti" = hanging) from the hill where the castle stands, or, finally, to the legend that one Alexander Iraklidis, a local feudal lord, hanged himself and his daughter from a tree on this hill when he lost his fief (16th century). This low hill, in the centre of the village to the left of the road, is crowned by the small church of Agios Nikolaos and the ruins of the small medieval castle of Kremasti. In the white Church of the Panagia, built on the site of an older church, there is a miraculous icon of Panagia Katholiki, whose saint's-day celebration is held every 10-23 August. If you are able to attend, you will have the opportunity to admire one of the performances given on all holidays by folk-dance troupes. A national handicraft exhibition is also held during August in the Commune's flower-garden. A gift from the "Elpis" Association of Kremasti natives in America has helped create an interesting library of 10,000 volumes in a handsome neo-classical building. Accord-

Opposite Page: The architecture of the houses is no less admirable when it is the work of anonymous craftsmen, as in this novel house in Kremasti.

90

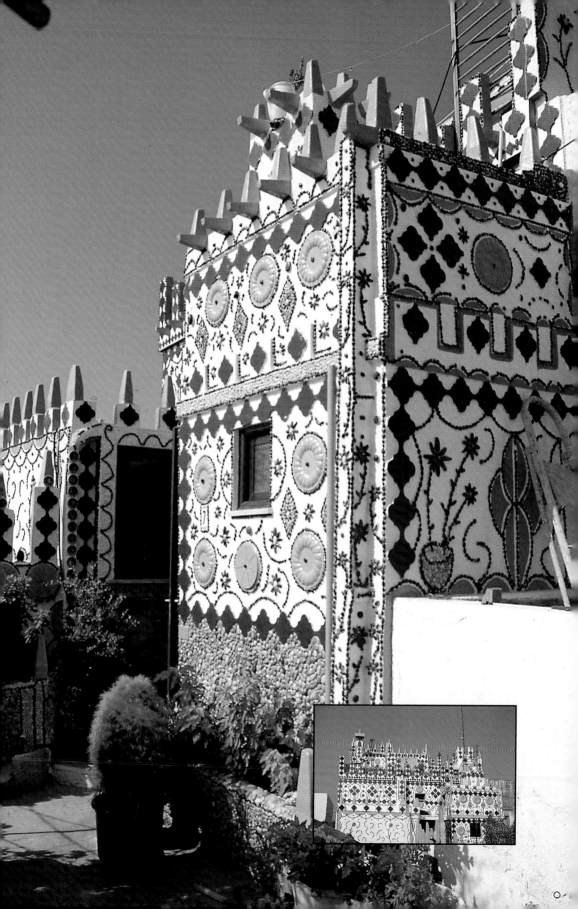

The stone Gymnasium building in Paradissi

ing to Strabo, Kremasti was an extension of ancient Ialysia. Remains of a Hellenistic workshop and graves from the Archaic period have been discovered in the area. From the Assomati area comes an impressive pithos-like amphora of the Early Bronze Age.

The seaside road continues on to **Paradissi**, site of the airport. Of note in the village itself are the stone Gymnasium building, the Commune, a traditional house that functions as a folklore museum, and the main Church of Agios Nikolaos, dating from 1900. In the village's environs are single-aisled basilicas housing frescos from the 13th-15th centuries [the Church of Agios Merkourios, the 15th-century Church of Agios Avakoum (Habakkuk, Old-Testament prophet of the 7th century BC), the Church of Agia Marina, and also the single-aisled basilicas of Agios Ioannis Theologos and Ipapanti at their namesake monasteries). Grand Master Villeneuve built a stronghold at the foot of Paradissi hill, site of the old village, which was from then on called Villanova in his honour. Today only a few ruins remain.

A turnoff to the left from the main road takes us to **Kalamonas**, renamed Peverango when Italians settled here (whereas under the Turks it had retained its Greek name), and to the quiet village of **Damatria**, which took its name from the goddess Demeter who may have been worshipped here. Before entering the vil-

lage, you will see the chapel of the Timios Stavros. The single-aisled basilica of Agia Paraskevi or Agios Nikitas, dating from the 12th century, is hollowed out of the side of Paradissi hill; its walls are graced by frescos from the latter half of the 13th century.

From here you can take the road to **Maritsa** and head for the Valley of the Butterflies. You will pass the well-built little Monastery of the Transfiguration and the chapel of Agios Georgios in a valley overgrown with fig-trees.

On the top of a hill are the ruins of the Church of Agios Nikolaos dating from 1453. You will end up at the **Valley of the Butterflies** (Kilada me tis Petaloudes; opening hours 9:00 am-sunset). Leave your car in the parking lot in front of the small tavernas and walk down to the valley (length 1 km., elevation 160-241 m.). Clinging to the Liquidambar trees (scientific name: Liquidambar orientalis) and to the rocks lining the stream are thousands of brightly-coloured moths. Members of the family of Lepidoptera, their scientific name is Callimorpha quadripunctaria, and they live out the rest of their life cycle far from the valley, in thickly-vegetated, damp areas of the island. They come to this valley only to mate. As adults they do not consume any food, and their small energy reserves make their migratory journey a hard one.

Despite an infinite number of signs telling visitors not to make noise and frighten the lovely insects which lose even more of the little energy left to them when forced to fly, some unscrupulous visitors shout, or, even worse, touch the moths! It is high time that man stopped behaving as though he were the only species entitled to live on this planet, and began to respect the moths, because if they leave the valley, this unique sight will be lost.

Opposite Page: The Valley of the Butterflies, in a riot of greenery and tourist indiscretions committed against the striped Lepidoptera

The Nativity of the Virgin in Psinthos

Two kilometres of passable dirt road run by Kalopetra Monastery, unfortunately closed. Dedicated to the Dormition of the Virgin, it stands on a hilltop with a splendid view of the sea, on the site of an older church built in 1782 by Alexander Ipsilantis

Agios Nektarios in Faliraki

Kalopetra Monastery

and later destroyed in an earthquake. As Ipsilantis was sailing to the Peloponnese, he was almost shipwrecked; he called on the Virgin for help and attributed his salvation to a miracle, whereupon he built the church.

The road continues on towards **Psinthos** (either devired from the absinthe or wormwood plant which grows in some abundance in the area, or a corruption of the name Sybithius). The village offers a few rooms for rent, and picturesque tavernas in a square pleasantly shaded by centenary plane-trees. Also on the square is the Church of the Nativity of the Virgin with the tall bell-tower. Ancient but depredated tombs were found in the area. Mt. Koutrobalos was the site of the decisive clash between the Italians and the Turks.

On the road to Arhipolis, in the courtyard of the Monastery of Agia Triada (called Iamatiki by the locals), built in 1407/8, a few remnants of a mosaic are all that remain of a basilica that once stood there. Two kilometres further on is the old 15th-century Monastery of Panagia Parmeniotissa, with important frescos. The bcchives to be seen around the village are a guarantee of the excellent quality of the honey produced here.

In the village of **Kalithies** you can see the old Church of the Transfiguration, built in 1891, with a notable 16th-century altar-screen. On the outskirts of the village lies the Monastery of Eleoussa whose church is a single-aisled basilica. The name of the village may be a corruption of its older name, Kallithea (= good view), or taken from the ancient Greek word "colythus" = hill. You can make short excursions into this area to see the Monastery of Agios Georgios, 2.5 km. from the village. A difficult footpath then leads to the cave of the same name, where evidence of human presence in the Neolithic Age (5,000-3,700 BC) has been discovered.

South of Kalithies, in the Mitropolitis locale, stands the single-aisled basilica of the Amos Monastery. Legend has it that the rocky islet of Katergo is nothing but a pirate ship, turned to stone by the Old-Testament, 8th-century BC prophet Amos, as it was preparing to put in to capture the islanders who were celebrating the prophet's name-day on 14/15th June.

Back on the coast road, you will see the impressive seaside tourist resort of **Faliraki**. An infinite number of luxury hotel units, shops of all kinds, a vibrant nightlife and a vast organised beach, with water shallow enough for children, where every-

Views of Faliraki resort, a veritable tourist paradise

The beach at Kalithea; its spa building a was designed in 1930 by the Italian architect Lombardi.

one engages in their favourite water sports with complete abandon, attract thousands of tourists each year.

On the road back to town you will pass **Kallithea**, with its famous healing springs, known already in the 7th-6th centuries BC for their purgative water, suitable for kidney and liver complaints. The spa installations were designed in 1930 by the talented Italian architect Pietro Lombardi. In addition to the Kallithea spring water, water was brought from the island of Kos to fill two heated tanks (Ippokrates and Agia Irini). Although the installations are no longer in operation, below the spa building are two beautiful little beaches combining sand and rocky shores, to which scores of visitors come by caique from Mandraki.

To the left of the coast road stands the lovely medieval village of **Koskinou**, known to have existed as far back as the 15th century. It took its name either from a landowner named Koskinas or from Koskinia in Asia Minor, whence its inhabitants came. (As you will observe in many other villages in the countryside, the names of political leaders have been preserved in Rhodes' place-names.) Walk through the village's narrow streets, in the quiet of the afternoon, and admire the

unique colourful façades of the houses, fine examples of popular neo-classicism. The old traditional houses are built on rectangular lots, each enclosed by a high wall with a gate. Opposite the gate is the house's single room, divided in the middle with an arch. This is where the whole family lived and slept.

Apart from the main Church of the Assumption, also worth visiting are the following single-aisled basilicas: Agios Loukas, Agios Ioannis, and cruciform Agia Irini. Mycenean tombs were discovered in this area. SW of the village are the ruins of a small castle.

In **(A)sgourou**, the houses are spread over an oak-clad hill, on the summit of which stands the Church of Agii Apostoli. Four groups of tombs from the 3rd century BC were excavated in this area, along with a cylindrical marble altar bearing Victories in bas-relief.

Left: *Interior of a traditional home in Koskinou*
Right: *The Church of Agios Ioannis Asgourou, built in 1450, and later converted into a mosque*
Below: *A stroll through the streets of the village of Koskinou will confirm its reputation as one of the island's most traditional villages.*

Local costume of Soroni, from the book The Dodecanese *by Athena Tarsouli*

Rhodes – Kamiros – Kritinia – Monolithos – Profitis Ilias

You will start out on the road you took in the previous excursion and follow an itinerary which includes almost all the villages of the ancient city-state of Camirus.

Head of a Silenus or Bacchus, from the Middle Hellenistic period (Rhodes Archaeological Museum).

Agios Spiridon, built in 1936 in Theologos

Just before Tholos, pre-war Italian excavations brought to light remains of the most noteworthy Doric sanctuary of Ialysia, built in the 4th century BC and dedicated to Apollo Erethimios, who had been worshipped since pre-Doric times as a protector of agriculture capable of warding off the disease of erysipelas. Also found here was a small 5th/4th-century BC theatre which was destroyed during World War II. On the hilltop in the tourist resort of **Theologos** or **Tholos**, with notable hotel units, stands the Church of Agios Spiridon, built in 1936, which once functioned as a monastery. Outside the village is the restored monastery of the same name.

In the picturesque village of **Soroni** (= place of many oak-trees) the 18th-century Monastery of Agios Loukas stands out among the white houses. A stop to see the lovely pine forest and the Monastery of Agios Sillas is a must. A single-aisled early Christian basilica dedicated to the saint was initially housed in a hollow in the rock; the water from the spring there was reputed to cure leprosy. In 1836 the fountain you now see outside was built. Lucky are those visitors whose visit coincides with the 10-day saint's-day celebration held at the monastery beginning on July 23rd. In the extensive area surrounding the monastery, with the picturesque little taverna, the playground and the playing fields, children and adults participate in sports and musical and dance events. (The locals live in the huts round about during this whole time!)

The conventual church of the Agios Sillas Monastery

The beach at Nea Kamiros

Close by is the village of **Fanes** [so named because formerly there was a beacon (= "fanos") here], with the Churches of Agios Ioannis and Agios Nikitas in the cemetery. On the outskirts of the village is the small Monastery of Agia Varvara, and in the direction of Kalavarda the old Monastery of the Transfiguration with the miraculous icon; it holds its saint's-day celebrations on August 6th. The road continues on to the hamlet of **Kalavarda**, which offers a few rooms to rent. It took its name from Vardas, a local dignitary and landowner. On the road to Salakos a Mycenean settlement and graveyard have been excavated. The Monastery of Agia Anna is on the same road; next to it is a ruined ancient tower which was later used as a water-mill.

On Cape Agios Minas – which in antiquity was named "Mylantia Akra" (= Mylantia Point) after the Mylantian gods – and near the waterfront at **Nea Kamiros** with its picturesque little tavernas, possibly the site of the ancient harbour, recent excavations have brought to light a settlement (Fig. IV, I), possibly the port town. The road runs up through a pine and oak forest to the site of the ancient city-state of Camirus, in area the smallest of the island's three, which is preserved in very good condition (opening hours 8:30 am-16:40 pm daily, 8:30 am-14:40 pm weekends, closed Mondays). Just before you reach the fenced-in archaeological site, you can see the foundations of an ancient temple and traces of other buildings (Fig. IV, II) on your left.

Camirus (from the Phoenician "kamirah" = place with clay-like, whitish soil) occupied the west central part of the island. The city (Fig. IV, III) is spread over the amphitheatre-like area where two convergent slopes rise to form a single flat summit. It was first inhabited in the Geometrical Era.

The Monastery of Agia Anna, and an ancient tower in ruins

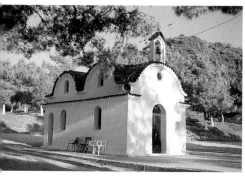

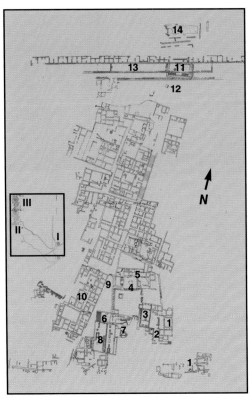

Figure IV: *Plan of the excavations at Kamiros, based on a topographical sketch by G. Konstantinopoulos*

Camirus is mentioned by Homer and Thucydides, because it was here that Diagorides Dorieus landed in 412/411 BC. Homer says that it was a colony set up by the son of Heracles and Iole, Camirus, but Pindar claims that Camirus was the son of Apollo. The inhabitants' main occupations were farming and stock-breeding, which brought them wealth. They minted coins bearing the image of a fig-leaf, on the standard of Aeginetan coinage, as they had limited commercial ties to the rest of the Aegean. The city seems never to have been walled. The destructive earthquake of 227/6 BC was the reason the city was rebuilt and remodelled. The earthquake of AD 142 is thought to have completely demolished it.

Reverberations of Mycenean installations on the island can be felt in the myth of Althaemenes, son of the Cretan King Catreus or Cretus. When Althaemenes learned that Catreus would be killed by one of his children, he was afraid that he might be the one, and went into self-exile on Rhodes. He founded a colony in Camirus which he called Cretinia. But because, as the ancient Greeks said, it is impossible to escape one's fate, Catreus lost his other children and sought out his only remaining heir in Rhodes. He arrived on the island at night and was so anxious to see him that he disembarked at once. But the islanders, thinking it was a pirate invasion, warned their King, who arrived with a guard and slaughtered the "invaders", including his own father. When he realised what he had done, he pleaded with the gods to put him under a curse. The ancient author Apollodorus (2nd century BC) relates that the earth opened up and swallowed him (Book III). Another myth has it that he voluntarily exiled himself in Ieron and that when he died he was worshipped by the inhabitants of Cretenia and Camirus.

The people of Camirus also worshipped the Mylantian gods, rural deities which originated in prehistoric times and were associated with mills and the grinding of grain.

The first excavations were carried out between 1852 and 1864 by the archaeologists and illegal dealers in antiquities, Alfred Biliotti and August Salzmann. From 1928 up to the World War II they were continued by Italian archaeologists.

The city was built like an amphitheatre on three levels. On the lowest were the public buildings. When you enter the site, as the ancients did, from the west side of the square, the first ruins you encounter are probably of private dwellings (Fig. IV, 1). In front of you spreads the flat surface of the square – to achieve this, a deep gouge had to be dug out of the SW slope, with retaining walls to support the rock face, and the north side banked up, with more retaining walls to hold in the earth.

To the buildings in the NE corner, which are on a higher level, belongs the Doric temple (Fig. IV, 3) dating from the 3rd-2nd centuries BC, with two columns between the antae at its entrance). It may have been dedicated to Pythian Apollo; the bases of the cult statue and the votive statues have been restored. Hollowed out of the floor at the rear of the base of the cult statue is a treasury; believers threw their obols into its holes! To the right of the temple is an Ionic temple-like building (Fig. IV, 2), and later buildings of unknown purpose. On its left are the Doric half-columns which formed the façade of a late Classical fountain (Fig. IV, 4) which has been partially restored. The water was dipped out of a long, narrow cistern in bronze cups. In the 3rd century BC, the cistern was replaced by a well, whose opening you see in the middle of this space. Behind the fountain are the remnants of a small stoa (Fig. IV, 5); in front of it is a square with a small square building and an inscribed stone on either side of its entrance. Finally, next to the staircase leading to the settlement's main street, are an exedra (Fig. IV, 7) and

The Doric temple, dating from the 3rd-2nd centuries BC. Behind it a sanctuary of the same epoch can be seen, with altars of deities.

a sanctuary (Fig. IV, 8) of the 3rd-2nd centuries BC, where altars of deities were ranged on two levels; below and to the SE of the sanctuary were older buildings.

On the middle level, above the slopes,

The restored Doric half-columns on the façade of the late Classical fountain

Part of the residential centre of Camirus and its main street

(Fig. IV, 10), of which six square columns, two antae and two columns of the atrium (inner courtyard) have been restored.

The uppermost level, i.e. the plateau on the summit (120 meters above sea level), was the site of the acropolis. You will see a cistern (Fig. IV, 11) of the 6th-5th centuries BC, which supplied water to 300-400 families during the dry season. It was probably covered, and had two sets of stairs so that it could be cleaned. This cistern, together with stone channels added in Hellenistic times and clay pipes during the Roman era, constituted the hydraulic system of the lower part of the city. A few meters before the cistern stands an altar (Fig. IV, 12) of porous stone. In the Middle Hellenistic Age a long, narrow, imposing stoa (Fig. IV, 13) was built in front of the sanctuary of Athena; it ran the whole length of the plateau (200 m.). Today some foundations remain of the two ranks of Doric columns, and of the apartments in the back, which probably served as accommodations for the pilgrims who came to attend religious

was the residential area. A restored Hellenistic staircase (Fig. IV, 6) led up to the settlement's main street (Fig. IV, 9). All the houses could be entered from the street. Cross-streets demarcated the building plots, in accordance with the Hippodamian system. At the northern end of the road there were baths, probably public, with tanks of water. At the point where the street becomes steps, you will see on your left a well-preserved, formerly two-story house

The residential centre on the pine-clad hillside, scattered with ancient remains, it slopes down to the sea. The restored square columns of a well-preserved house can be seen.

A cistern from the 6th-5th centuries BC, and the steps used when cleaning it

The partially-finished facade of a Lycian tomb in Kamiros Skala

festivals. The stylobate of the outer colonnade put the cistern out of use, and it was replaced by 16 wells, which were dug in the apartments of the stoa, along with an underground water supply system.

Further up are the foundations of the wall surrounding the sanctuary and the peripteral (having a row of columns on all four sides) Hellenistic temple of Athena Camiras (Polias, Fig. IV, 14). This was probably a tetrastyle Doric temple built on the site of an older Classical temple, when the latter was demolished in the 227/6 BC earthquake.

The inhabitants' love for beautiful pottery and kouroi can be seen in the grave goods unearthed in the extensive Geometric and Archaic cemeteries on the hills round about (at Papa tis Loures, Kehraki, Pateles, Galatomilos, Makri Langoni and Fikeloura).

On the coast road you will pass several beaches and the hamlet of **Mandriko**, before reaching the seaside village of **Kamiros Skala**, with picturesque tavernas serving fresh fish. Caiques sail from here to the neighbouring island of Halki. ("Skala" was the name for the warehouses built in the harbouro corving inland settlements. In time they grew into small settlements in their own right.) The area was inhabited from ancient times, and was associated with the mythical Cretan here Althaemenes. Its ruins were inundated by the sea. A partially finished façade of a Ly-

cian tomb and an early Christian basilica with a mosaic which stood on the beach were destroyed by the waves. The Byzantine buildings that remained were torn down so that their materials could be used to construct or repair defence works.

Southwest of Kamiros Skala, the main point of interest is the rectangular castle of Kritinia, the **Kastello** (from the Latin castel-

At the propylaea were the marble basins which held water for the purification of the pilgrims before they entered the temple. This basin was discovered in Kamiros and dates from the 7th century BC (Rhodes Archaeological Museum).

lum or the Castel Nuovo mentioned in 1480). On the two round towers were the coats of arms of Grand Masters d'Amboise and Caretto, and on the castle's south wall those of Grand Masters d'Aubusson and Orsini. Inside the castle are the ruins of the Catholic Church of St. Paul. The castle was used by the Italians as a dockyard. The fallen debris and the shrubbery, which has grown up all around the castle, make it impossible to get to. The footpath will take you to its gate, from which you will have a unique view of the sea.

According to the Florentine scholar, cleric and traveller, Cristoforo Buondelmonti, there were several Byzantine castles on the western coast of Rhodes. We do not know, however, whether the Kastello was still standing when he visited the island (1412-1420). In 1479, the Knights, in possession of various information about an impending attack by Mahomet II, were in a continual state of preparation, and issued decrees determining which castle the in-habitants of each castle were to take refuge in. The people needed special permission to go out and harvest their crops and bring them into the castle.

After touring the castle, you can let the sea "wash away" the day's fatigue, and have a meal at one of the little tavernas on the waterfront.

In post-Byzantine times, the seaside settlement of Skala moved inland, to the mountain village of **Kritinia**, which was known as Kastello up to 1945 because of the castle of the same name. In this picturesque village, do not fail to visit the Kritinia Folklore Museum housed since 1993 in a modern round building. At the Amartos locale is the chapel of the Panagia, which celebrates with festivals on September 8 and the Tuesday after Faster. Nearby stands a partially ruined Crusader building.

A turnoff to the right from the main road leads through vineyards to **Stelies**, and continues on to the beach at Glifada, where a couple of tavernas set their tables

The rectangular castle of Kritinia, Kastello

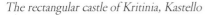

out on the sands, and then to the Monastery of Zoodohos Pigi. The road by-passes Akramitis or Gramithi (823 m.), nestled in thick vegetation, and winds up at the isolated rocky crag crowned by one of the Knights' four most impregnable strongholds, the castle of Monolithos (= huge single rock). It was built in 1476 by Grand Master d'Aubusson over the ruins of a small Byzantine castle. Its striking appearance will leave you breathless, as it does the dozens of visitors who stop here on the road at all times of day to photograph it. You will leave your car and climb up to the castle by the stone staircase. None of the ruins has been identified, apart from the single-aisled basilica of Agios Pandeleimon. The best time of day to visit the castle is in the evening, when the sun is sinking into the sea and the rocks of the stronghold are painted red.

Back to reality, and to the traditional village of Monolithos, with one hotel and a few rooms for rent: The roofs of the older houses are plastered with "patelia", a spe-

The castle of Monolithos reaches up in a desperate attempt to touch the sky

The Kritinia folklore museum, opened in 1993, and some of its exhibits

105

View of Monolithos. The roofs of the older houses are insulated with "patelia".

cial mixture of earth, oil and salt which forms a crust, making the roof water-tight and insulating it against the heat. On the first Sunday after Easter, at the name-day celebration of Agios Thomas, honour is paid to the memory of the village's heroes of the Resistance Struggle against the Germans.

A 6th-century BC grave in this area

Above: *Agios Pandeleimon in Siana*
Below: *The restored Monastery of Agios Ioannis Theologos Artamitis*

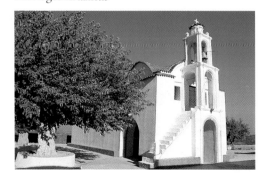

yielded cinerary urns. This form of burial, where the body was first cremated and then placed in an urn or ossuary, was common in Rhodes during the Geometric and early Archaic periods. The custom of cremation demonstrates the dependence of the Rhodian centres on Attica. On the lovely beaches of Fourni with the strange rock formations, excavations in 1905 brought to light burials in openings in the rocks. (These rocks may have provided shelter for fishermen from the surrounding ancient settlements.) NE of Monolithos is the single-aisled basilica of the Monastery of Agia Anastassia. Another old monastery is the one dedicated to the Prophet Habakkuk, in the Vassilikos locale. On the road to Siana is the single-aisled basilica of Agios Georgios.

The next village is tiny **Siana** with the single-aisled basilica of Agios Pandeleimon. The name Siana is a corruption of the name of the ancient township of Brasiannae or Brasiae. The villagers are justly proud of their pure honey from flowers, thyme and pine-blossoms, and of the local spirits known as "souma" which they distil from locally-grown grapes. A turnoff to the right from the main road leads past the sad spectacle of a burned forest, to the traditional village of Agios Issidoros with its namesake church. In the village's old cemetery stands a one-aisled basilica. On the road to Embona, you will encounter the restored whitewashed Monastery of Agios Ioannis Theologos Artamitis. As the Knights took no particular care to impose their own ideology on the island, this monastery, built in the 9th-10th centuries, was an important centre of Greek studies. A Byzantine scholar who visited it in 1233 wrote that it had a well-stocked library. During the Turkish occupation, it functioned as a school for priests until the Turks demolished it and the monastery seen today was built. It celebrates its name-day with festivities on September 26th. In touristy **Embona**, see the Church of the Panagia and

View of traditional Embona, the Monastery of Agios Georgios, and the library

the small Monastery of Agios Georgios. Don't leave this village without tasting the excellent local wine at one of the friendly little tavernas; you may also buy one of an infinite number of colourful embroideries. Some of the villagers still wear their traditional costumes. The name Embona is probably derived from the word "ambon" (= mountain peak). The imposing bare mountain you can see from here is Atavyros (elevation 1,215 m.; it was one of the first mountains to be measured). Nature-lovers will be enchanted by its rich flora and fauna. For those with the time, inclination and above all stamina, there is a footpath at the foot of the mountain which leads up to the sanctuary of Atavyrian Zeus. Limited excavations in 1927 revealed inscriptions and rich dedications, and proved that the sanctuary continued in use up to Roman times. As to the bronze oxen/dedications at the sanctuary, it was said that, when some strange event was about to happen, they would start to bellow! Theors (= sacred envoys) gathered here from all three of Rhodes' ancient cities.

Interior of a house in Embona. Anyone would think it was the work of an experienced interior designer!

Local costume of Salakos, from the book The Dodecanese *by Athena Tarsouli*

Althaemenes, the mythical hero who colonised Camirus, introduced the worship of Zeus from Crete and built a temple in his honour on Mt. Atavyros; from it on a clear day he could see Mt. Ida in his homeland. As he wrote his Olympian Ode in sight of Mt. Atavyros, Pindar begged the father of the gods to receive his hymn and to protect the house of the Diagoridae.

Salakos, with houses clinging to the hillside and fragrant, well-tended gardens, took its name from a landowner of that name. Sports lovers can visit the athletic installations including football fields and tennis, basketball and volleyball courts. Worth seeing in the village is the 14th-century Church of the Assumption. In the village square a portion of the enceinte of the Crusader castle remains. On the road to Embona, excavations were recently carried out on the ruins of the early Christian, 5th-century church known as "Paleoeklissia", with a mosaic floor. In the opposite direction is the Nymphi spring, which supplies part of the water for Rhodes town. From here a footpath leads up to the stone chapel of Archangelos. Just below the spring, rare butterfly species live in an un-

On the fir-clad peak of Mt. Profitis Ilias stands the Church of Profitis Ilias.

The "Elafos" and "Elafina" Hotels

touched wooded area.

The road winds up the splendid mountain of **Profitis Ilias** (elevation 870 m.), where the trees grow so thickly that they block out the sun. A narrow staircase leads to a ruined stone Catholic chapel whose façade bears a bas-relief of St. George and the Dragon. The stone-paved footpath winds up at the ruined Villa de Vecchi where official personages once stayed; it is now state property. Lower down are the disused "Elafos" and "Elafina" Hotels (which belong to the "Astir" Hotel) and the Church of Profitis Ilias, where the Prophet Elijah is pictured on a winged chariot like that of the Sun. The Church holds its saint's-day celebrations on July 19th.

From here a passable dirt road leads to **Apollona**, a traditional Rhodian village, which probably took its name from a temple dedicated to the ancient god Apollo, the remains of which were discovered in the courtyard of the village's fine folklore

The outstanding folklore museum in Apollona

museum, which includes a library of some note. In this same area there are ruins of the Byzantine castle; from its top, Lindos is said to be visible. The winding lanes will take you to the Church of the Holy Cross, housing a rare manuscript Gospel, written on vellum, an icon showing the Prophet Elijah on a winged chariot similar to the sun god's, and a piece of the Holy Cross, which tradition has it was brought to Rhodes by St. Helen herself. It is also said

The icon of Panagia Kariona with the arms of d'Aubusson

that the church's carved wooden altar-screen took 8-9 years to make! Outside the village there is a lovely little wooded park with picnic tables. In the wayside chapel of Panagia Kariona, two km. outside the village, the icon of the Virgin bears the arms of d'Aubusson.

On the mountainside, among the Calabrian Pines (Pinus brutia), stand the houses of the village of **Platania**. In the Church of Agios Georgios, built in 1850,

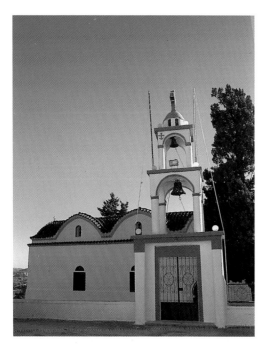

Agios Georgios in Platania

see the fine carved wooden altar screen. Four kilometres further on, you will come to

Agios Nikolaos in Foundoukli, with unique Byzantine frescos

Offices and shops used by the Italians during their stay in Eleoussa

Eleoussa, site of the monastery of the same name. Around the imposing Church of Agios Haralambos (formerly Catholic) are the houses, offices and shops used by the Italians during their stay in the area (at that time it was known as Campochiaro). Most of them were woodcutters who exploited the nearby forest and were subsidised by the Italian state. After another two kilometres on a road lined with centenary plane-trees, you will arrive at Koskinistis spring. Here is the stone 13th-century chapel of Agios Nikolaos at **Foundoukli**, with four apses and unique Byzantine frescos dating from the 14th or 15th centuries. They were restored by the Italians.

In the small hamlet of **Dimilia** (= two mills), with many plane-trees and the two mills that gave it its name, see the basilica of Zoodohos Pigi next to the spring of the same name. It is said that its icon of the Virgin was found on a nearby mountain.

Zoodohos Pigi in Dimilia

The beach of Ladiko or Antony Quinn

Afandou Bay and Kolimbia, as seen from the Monastery of Tsambika

Rhodes – Epta Piges – Archangelos – Faraklos

The following two itineraries include most of the villages of the ancient city-state of Lindia. You will leave town on the road to Lindos. After Faliraki, a turnoff to the left leads to the beach known as **Ladiko** or **Antony Quinn**, formed by two small stretches of sand and a few rocks.

Further to the south and off to the right from the main road is **Afandou** (ancient township of Brygindariae), developed for tourism, but still a village with strong Rhodian colour. It might not be off the mark to believe that it owes its name (afandou = unseen) to the fact that it is not visible from the sea and thus safe from pirates. It is also said to have taken its name from a feudal lord named Euphantus. In the square is the three-aisled Church of the Assump-

The Church of the Panagia Katholiki in Afandou, built on the site of an early Christian basilica; it houses fine frescos

The Dormition of the Virgin in Afandou

Agios Nektarios in Arhipoli

tion/Agios Loukas/Tris Ierarhes, dating from 1839, whose bell-tower was added in 1924. It houses an interesting folklore exhibition including local costumes, models of rooms in Rhodian houses, etc. (opening hours 9:00-11:30 am and 4:00-6:00 pm daily). There is also a rug-making workshop, where you may buy gorgeous rugs. To the left of the main road, towards the sea, is the stone Church of the Monastery of Panagia Katholiki, built in the 17th century, with a whitewashed façade and 17th/18th-century frescos. The churchyard wall was built of materials taken from the early Christian basilica of the 5th or 6th century which once stood on this site. (Note the four limestone column capitals.) Golf and water-sport aficionados will particurarly appreciate the golf course and cosmopolitan beach on Afandou Bay.

On this route you will encounter another of the wonders of Rhodian nature, the **Valley of Epta Piges** ("Seven Springs"),

with lush vegetation. The water flows out from the stone dam, and some of it goes through a tunnel 186 m. long and winds up in a small lake. The tunnel continues on through the mountain; it was built by the Italians to supply water to Kolimbia. More staid visitors will limit themsclves to a good meal at one of the valley's shady tavernas, while the adventurous will take off their shoes and wade into the tunnel to admire the unique lake.

Five kilometres inland lies **Arhipoli**, with a few rooms to rent. Your attention will be drawn to the Church of Agios Nektarios and the spring in the shade of a huge old plane-tree. Also of note is the stone Church of Agios Dimitrios with the handsome bell-tower, 200 years old. Cross the main road and take the road lined with eucalyptus trees that runs through the tourist resort of **Kolimbia** (from the ancient Greek word "Colympus" = depression containing stationary water). The area was renamed

It is strange that more people are not familiar with the Valley of the Seven Springs.

San Benedetto under the Italians, who tried to create a model community there. This area has everything a visitor could want, in addition to two lovely little bays suitable for water sports.

From the main road, the large white-washed building complex of the Monastery of Panagia Paramithia can be seen on the mountain opposite. Building on it began in 1989, and its conventual church contains portable icons as well as important frescos.

On the right side of the main road stands the large **Monastery of Panagia Tsambika** or **Kira**. It was built around the 16th century to serve pilgrims to the small monastery that crowns the peak of the conical hill opposite. In its stone-paved courtyard with the shady cypress-tree and the spring, a traditional saint's-day celebration is held on September 8th. (Some visitors can be accommodated in the monastery's cells.) You can drive up the

The Panagia Paramithia Monastery

hill (elevation 287 m.) as far as the little café, and continue on foot. The church you see was built approximately 700 years ago, and restored in 1760. It has splendid interior decoration as well as a miraculous icon of the Annunciation of the Virgin.

The islanders erroneously trace the etymology of the name "Tsambika" or "Sambika" to the word "tsamba" (= spark, flame). Their mistake stemmed from the

Agios Trifonas, in the courtyard of the home for the aged in Kolimbia

The eucalyptus-lined road leads to the long beach of Kolimbia.

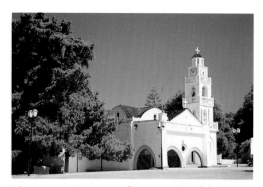

The newer Monastery of Panagia Tsambika or Kira, next to the main road

following religious tradition referring to the strange way the miraculous icon left Cyprus and came to be found here: One evening a shepherd saw a flame coming from a cypress-tree on the hill. He thought it was another shepherd, and watched to see whether it would move. The same thing happened several evenings in a row, and finally the shepherd and his company armed themselves, out of fear of the un-

known, and went up the hill. To their great surprise they saw before them the silver icon illuminated by a votive light. The rumour of the miracle reached the Monastery of our Lady of Cyprus, and, as was only natural, a committee was sent to get the miraculous icon. But it returned to Rhodes, and that night the shepherd saw it shining on the hill again. Once again the Cypriots took it to their island, and once again it returned to Rhodes. Then, to be sure it was the same icon, the Cypriots burned one side of it a little – the mark can still be seen. The icon came back again, and then finally the Cypriots decided it was God's will that a church be built to house it. Later a monastery was built around it.

The view from the monastery is indescribable, but even more memorable is the fine beach at Tsambika, at the foot of the hill.

The next village you come to is the traditional market town of **Archangelos**, with any number of places to visit, all of which

View of the old Monastery of Tsambika, and the beach at the foot of its hill

The Church of the Archangel, metropolis of the town of Archangelos. In the background its Crusader castle can be seen.

the hill above it; the castle was continued by his successor, Zacosta and finished by Orsini.

Outstanding among the old churches is the settlement's main church, that of the Archangel Gabriel Patitiriotis [because, according to the folk tradition, he presses ("pato" = press) people to remove their souls when they die, or because he used to help the villagers press their grapes]. Another is the Church of the Taxiarhis, dating from 1800; it is the settlement's metropolis, dedicated to the Archangel Gabriel, who is the village's patron. Others include Agios Antonios, Profitis Ilias and the one-aisled basilica of Panagia Alemonitra. Also of note is the Monastery of Agios Ioannis, with ruined 15th-century frescos.

Despite its 1,632 beds and other tourist amenities, Archangelos still retains its traditional atmosphere. Of the dozens of ceramic workshops, only that of Panagiotis Papouras on the road to Stegna is still in op-

The works of man have given Archangelos' houses a special beauty.

confirm a constant human presence from ancient times to the present. In the small cave of Koumelos (area 1,400 square meters) the speliologist Petrohilou discovered stone tools from the Middle Palaeolithic Era and potsherds from the Late Neolithic Era, as well as chick-peas, grains of wheat and a human skeleton. The cave is on the road to Stegna, and although it has not been developed, one can visit it. A marble plaque unearthed in this area informs us that this was the site of the ancient settlement of Ialysia, Pontoreia. Mycenean tombs were found in the area. Because of repeated pirate invasions, all the villages round about coalesced into a single settlement, Archangelos, which quickly began to prosper. In 1457, in the face of a terrible invasion by the Turkish fleet, Grand Master Jacques de Milly (1454-1461) fortified the village by building the majestic castle on

The old rustic houses with their masonry ovens (above), and the Church of Agios Georgios dating from 1830 (below), in Malona

eration. There is also a small rug-making establishment. During the week of cultural events scheduled for August 12th to 20th, you can watch traditional music and dance performances in Archangelos, put on by the local folkdance troupe and philharmonic. The luckiest visitors, who are able to attend a local wedding, will sample the "koulouria", made out of a type of dough with cheese. The road winds up at the lovely beach and little harbour of Stegna.

Outside town on the main road to Lindos, do not miss the Monastery of Agii Theodori, built in the year 1000. The Byzantine frescoes of 1372 were covered over with two inches of plaster applied by the village women who were unaware of their rarity. In Petrona, see the Church of Agios Georgios Petroniatis with important painted decoration of the 15th century.

A turnoff to the right leads through a fertile valley with olive orchards, vegetable gardens and forests of plane-trees and cypresses. In traditional **Malona** (= fertile place, from the ancient Greek "meleon"), see the old rustic houses from the early 19th century, with flower-filled gardens and masonry ovens. Important sights in the village are the beautiful Church of the Transfiguration with a 19th-century bell-tower containing stained-glass windows, and the Church of Agios Georgios, dating from 1830, which also has a fine bell-tower, built in 1890. The village's picturesqueness is rounded out by the chapels of the Exaltation of the Holy Cross and of the Evangelistria.

The road runs on to **Massari**, whose inhabitants get on with their lives unperturbed by the legions of tourists that tramp through their island each year. Visit the Church of the Presentation of the Virgin Mary, built in 1908, the Elementary School of 1918, no longer in use, and the single-aisled basilica of Panagia Kaminariotissa. It is said that sugar cane was once cultivated in this area. The village suffered severe earthquakes several times during the 19th century. A turnoff to the right from the main road to Lindos takes you to the Monastery of Taxiarhi in Kamiri, with a mosaic floor and fine frescos. Around the courtyard shaded by a grapevine are the cells, which fill up with pilgrims for the Monastery's name-day celebrations on July 13th.

The road continues to the beach of

The Presentation of the Virgin and the Elementary School in Massari

Malona and the newly-built village of **Haraki**, with a few rooms to rent. Below the castle, a mill was discovered which had been part of a sugar refinery in operation up to the time of the Knights. On the summit of a small hill 150 m. in height, stand the ruins of the mighty castle of Faraklos (whose name means "bald", a reference to the bald hill), or Feraclo, as the Knights called it. From the ancient coins and potsherds found here, we may assume that it was the site of the acropolis of some township during antiquity. In Byzantine times, a fortress was built to fend off pirates, and it fell to the Knights in September of 1306, after three days of resistance by the Byzantine garrison. After the invasion of 1444, the Knights became conscious of the need to restore the Byzantine castles in the countryside. In 1470, Grand Master Orsini began to repair Faraklos, and until 1479 it was one of the island's four main strongholds. Today's visitor will see only the portal, the enceinte, a few demolished walls of the church and the troops' quarters, and a square cistern for collecting water. The icon of the Panagia of Apollona was brought here to keep it from falling into the hands of the Turks.

The mighty castle of Faraklos

In the village square stands the Church of the Apostles – St. Paul is said to have stopped here. After a swim at the white pebble beach, you can have a meal in one of the little tavernas. South of the beach are the fenced-off traces of an ancient settlement.

Outside Haraki, a dirt road leads off to the left to the early Christian Church of Agia Agathi, in a hollow in the rock face. Next to it is a large cave, and below a beautiful beach.

After several kilometres you will arrive at **Kalathos** (a corruption of Clasioe, the ancient township of Lindus), with a few hotels and a good number of rooms to rent.

View of newly-built Haraki with its pebble beach

The vast beach lining Vliha Bay

The Convent of Ipseni

In the ruins of the Church of Agios Ioannis, stones from an ancient olive-press were found in 1903. One important church is the domed basilica of Agios Georgios in Kapi. Now it is time for a swim at the vast beach in Vliha Bay. The area was used during the Middle Ages as farming and grazing land for Lindos. The Danish archaeologists Johannes K.F. Kinch and C. Blinkenberg discovered a Roman altar here in 1902. Two hundred meters from the beach, see the Church of Panagia tis Evlo, hollowed out of the rock, with wall-paintings from the 13th century.

A turnoff to the right leads to **Pilona**, where rural life continues untouched by time. On a low hill at the entrance to the village stands the old Church of the Annunciation. In 1914 Kinch found gold jewellery here in two Geometric-Era graves. The village suffered severe damage in the 1926 earthquake. Also in this area is the domed, single-aisled basilica of Agia Kira.

Agios Georgios in Lardos

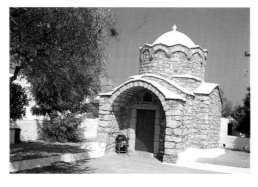

The road continues on towards **Lardos**, which offers a few rooms to rent. In the Exohi locale, Danish archaeologists discovered an ancient quarry from which red and black stone was taken. Five hundred meters south of the village on a low hill are the foundations of the enceinte and towers of the Byzantine castle of Lardos. The castle and the village were given in 1309 as a fief to the last Genoan lord of Rhodes, Admiral Vignoli, for helping them take the island. His descendants kept them until 1404, when they passed to the Knights, who did not make any changes or improvements to the castle. The single-aisled basilica of Panagia Katholiki, with 17th- and 18th-century frescos, was built on the foundations of an older basilica from the 5th-6th century, one kilometre south of the village. Also to the south is the single-aisled basilica of Agios Ioannis.

A narrow asphalt-paved road runs through the pine forest, a section of which has unfortunately burned, to the Convent of Ipsenis, with a tall white bell-tower, in a forest of pines, cypresses and myrtle. It is said to owe its name to the icon of the Virgin found in plaster ("gypsos"). Notice the carved wooden iconostasis and the old frescos. On the hill of Golgotha opposite stands a huge cross. This monastery, along with Tharri Monastery, offers hospitality to children from war-torn and Third World countries.

Four kilometres after **Laerma** (ancient

Overall view of Laerma

The sandy beach at Pefki

Ladarma – a pre-Hellenic place-name meaning people of Hermes, perhaps because that god was worshipped here), with the Church of Agios Georgios standing on a hillock, a passable dirt road brings as to the Byzantine Monastery of the Archangel Michael in Tharri. In the stone conventual church, see the carved wooden altar-screen of 1756 and the large icon of the Archangel. The fine frescos, in many layers, were painted in the 12th-16th centuries. Around the stone-paved courtyard

are the monastery's newly-built cells. NE of Tharri, in the Erimokastello locale, near the Monastery of Agios Georgios, there are ruins of an old building.

You will retrurn to Lardos, and visit the new settlement of **Pefki**, with a few hotels and rooms to rent, nice restaurants and tavernas, and a string of excellent beaches. During the Middle Ages, the area was used as farming and grazing land for Lindos.

The Monastery of the Archangel Michael in Tharri, with important frescos

Rhodes – Lindos

This chapter is not an itinerary like the previous ones. It includes only the area's chief point of interest, **Lindos**. In the description that follows you will realise why it was necessary to dedicate a special section to the area. Besides, as the area is so enchanting, few people will want to end their holidays without having spent at least a few days here.

The city-state of Lindia was the island's largest in area. Lindos, whose name is pre-Hellenic and means "rock", was in existence as early as the 9th or 10th century BC. Homer mentions that its first settler was the son of Helios, Cercaphus, where-

as Pindar and Strabo contend that he was the son of Cercaphus, Lindos. In the island's most protected bay Rhodes' most important harbour was established, and great progress was made in shipping and shipbuilding (according to the ecclesiastical author Eusebius, the Lindians built a special type of ship, the "Lindicon"). In the 6th century BC they minted coins bearing the emblem of the lion's head, according to the Phoenician standard, to facilitate trade with the Phoenicians and Egyptians.

Whereas the other city-states of Rhodes were gradually abandoned after the new city was founded in 408/7 BC, Lindos remained famous for its sanctuary of

Panoramic view of Lindos, its bay, and the rock of its acropolis, looming over the sea. The first sight

Lindian Athena up to early Roman times. Constant pirate invasions forced the islanders to abandon shipping in the 6th century and to retreat into the castle until the 13th century, when the Church of St. John was built. From the 13th-14th centuries on, a new settlement began to be built under the acropolis, over the ruins of the ancient city, around the patch of level ground, invisible from the sea, where the Church of the Panagia stood, and commerce and shipping began to develop once again.

The ancient city of Lindus extended down from the acropolis. Space for building was severely limited, and thus there was no room for town-planning or creation of a grid of streets, even during Hellenistic times, when such changes were being made in Rhodes' other cities. During that period, public buildings stood at either end of the harbour, with the residential area in between. On the site of today's square with the spring there was a smaller patch of level ground, where the ancient inhabitants went to get their water, as did the modern villagers until a regular water supply network was installed in 1965. The buses and taxis that connect Lindos with the rest of the island stand in that square. (You can leave your car in the parking lot above the two harbours.) The square is also the terminus for the donkeys – the

ctable will leave you breathless (1853 engraving by Flandin).

You can ascend the acropolis on foot or on donkey-back – here you can forget the four-wheeled monsters of the town!

town's only "means of transport" (you may find them useful for getting up to the acropolis)! It also serves as an "agora", as the older men gather here to discuss the day's events, and as a venue for saints'-day festivals. The square and the street, the settlement's broadest, that linked it to the place where the Church of the Panagia stands today, continue to be the nerve-centres of today's settlement.

In addition to providing accommodation in rented rooms, and nightlife in 28 bars (with respect for the permanent residents), Lindos guarantees a restaurant for every palate, with over 32 to choose from. As to shopping, there are shops in the square as well as under the acropolis. Best sellers are the elaborate dishes and remarkable hand-embroidered items.

The first to show an interest in the acropolis of Lindos was the German archaeologist and traveller Ludwig Ross, Ephor of Antiquities under King Otho, who visited Lindos in 1843 and persuaded the Turks to give him a few days to record the inscriptions on the wall of the sacred precinct and on the bases of the statues. His collaborator, the architect Loren, made drawings of the ancient monuments. Excavations were first (1902-1914) carried out in Lindos by the Danish archaeologists Kinch and Blinkenberg, and later (1952) by another Danish archaeologist, Ejnar Dyggve. The acropolis was restored by the Ital-

ians before the Second World War. Thus what today's visitor sees are monuments that have been reconstructed using architectural elements of local porous stone.

Before proceeding to a description of the site, the visitor must be made aware that the buildings on the acropolis were built in stages. In brief, we can state that the oldest finds date from Neolithic and Mycenean times, that the temple, sanctuary, wall and a rough staircase were built in the Archaic Era, that the propylaea and large staircase date from the 4th century BC, the large stoa from the Hellenistic epoch, the cisterns and vaults from late Hellenistic times, and the Church of St. John and the house of the captain of the guard from the Byzantine era: the latter was converted into an administrative headquarters in the time of the Knights (opening hours 8:00 am-18:00 pm daily, 8:30 am-14:45 pm weekends, closed Mondays). In more detail:

The footpath that leads up to the entrance to the outer wall has been in the same place since the Archaic period, but was restored and rebuilt during Hellenistic and Byzantine times. Today's visitor will use it to climb up to the acropolis, just as the ancient worshipper did. The only difference is that today amiable ladies display their embroidery on its paving stones! After climbing the few steps (Fig. V, 1), you will find yourself on a patch of level ground with cisterns (Fig. V, 2) for collecting water and a few scrawny trees. Lucius Aelius Anglochartus, priest at the temple of Lindian Athena during Roman times, carved an inscription in the Lindian rock where he boasts of his achievement in adorning the sanctuary with olive-trees. On the next level you see before you an exedra (Fig. V, 3) hollowed out of the rock, on the back of which the same priest carved the second out of a total of five inscriptions. Behind it a section of the Byzantine fortifications (Fig. V, 4) can be seen. On its right, in bas-relief on the rock, is the stern of an ancient ship

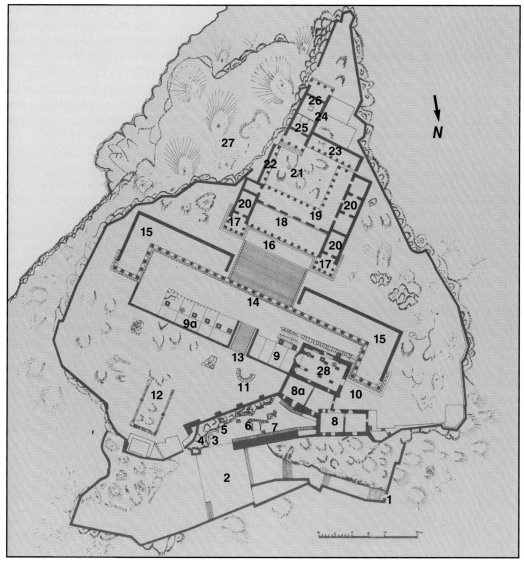

Figure V: *Topographical plan of the acropolis of Lindos, based on a drawing by G. Konstantinopoulos and Holger Rasmussen*

(Fig. V, 5), where in the second century BC a statue by the sculptor Pythocritus was erected in honour of an admiral, Hagesander, son of Mikion.

The acropolis covers an area of 8,380 square meters. It is not known whether the castle is the work of his Byzantine predecessors, or whether it was restored by Grand Master Villaret when he and his supporters took refuge in Lindos after a

dispute within the order. (It is said that they intended to arrest him because his way of life was considered to be scandalous!) A steep staircase (Fig. V, 7) – the work of Grand Master Fluvian or Grand Master d'Aubusson, whose coat of arms graces a window in the administration building – leads to the portal of the Crusader castle; on its left are traces of the ancient stairs (Fig. V, 6) that were connected to an entrance at the side of the present one. The building you see on your left is the administration building (Fig. V, 8, 8a), former residence of the Byzantine captain of the guard, which was rebuilt in 1317 by Villaret and restored late in the 15th century by d'Aubusson.

Entering the castle gate, you come into the first vaulted space on the ground floor of the administration building (Fig. V, 8), with ancient statue bases and altars. It was built there for defence purposes (Above the entrance is a "meurtrière", a ledge from which boiling water or oil was poured on attackers). On the inside it was adorned with inscriptions and wall-paintings, a section of which remains above the fireplace in the hall furthest to the south. (Ross saw wall-paintings with blue and gold lilies, garlands, landscapes, etc.) On the way out you turn left. The restored wall (Fig. V, 10) which you now see was part of the large Hellenistic stoa. Next you enter the second vaulted ground-floor area in the administration building (Fig. V, 8a). (Its guard and the few inhabitants who remained in the castle until the beginning of the 20th century were forced to move when their homes were torn down in the 1902 excavations.) As you leave, on your right you encounter three spacious restored vaults (Fig. V, 9) of the late Hellenistic era. After the staircase, seven more, smaller vaults (Fig. V, 9a) continue in the same direction, together creating the base for a spacious terrace.

Just before the stairs, on your left, upon a base of rough stone is an exedra (Fig. V, 11) made of local grey marble. Here, the inscription tells us, the well-known sculptor Phyles, son of Polygnotus from Halicarnassus, was commissioned by the wealthy family of one Pamphilidas, priest of Athens, to erect his statue. Smaller statues

Left: *At the foot of the staircase there are an exedra carved out of the rock and the stern of an ancient ship, where the statue of an admiral stood. Behind it a section of the Byzantine fortifications can be seen.*
Right: *The stairs leading up to the castle (1853 engraving by Flandin). Next to them the remains of the ancient staircase can be seen.*

124

of eminent members of the same family were added during the first century BC and the first century AD. In the area that opens up on your left there are pedestals from offerings to the sanctuary, and near the wall the foundations of a Roman temple. From here the "tomb of Cleobulus" can be seen on the tip of the rocky peninsula opposite.

Climb the stairs (Fig. V, 13) and you will encounter the restored 3rd-century BC Doric stoa (Fig. V, 15), built in the shape of a rectangle open at one end; it occupied almost the whole width of the acropolis. Of its 42 columns, 20 have been restored. In the middle of the back side, the wall had an opening, although the colonnade was not interrupted, to allow the great staircase of the propylaea to pass through. In the spacious square that opens up in front of the stoa there are numerous bases which once supported offerings to the temple. Rainwater ran off the acropolis buildings and was collected in cisterns dug in the first century BC out of the rock in front of the stoa. On your right, over the cisterns and vaults, stand the ruins of the Byzan-

The wall which supported the Hellenistic stoa

tine Church of St. John (Fig. V, 28), dating from the 13th century. It is three-aisled domed church of the cross-in-the-square type. The older foundations surrounding it probably belong to a 5th- or 6th-century Early Christian basilica which once stood here. [In drawings by one of Kinch's colleagues, Hans Koch, the mihrab (prayer niche indicating the direction of Mecca) created when the church was converted into a mosque can be seen.]

From the propylaea staircase (Fig. V, 14), built over its Archaic predecessor, you ascend to the sanctuary's highest level,

Left: *A vaulted space on the ground floor of the administrative building, with ancient inscribed bases and altars*
Right: *The exedra where the statue of Pamphilidas stood*

The Byzantine Church of Agios Ioannis

the temenos of Athena. The stairs and propylaea date from the 4th century BC. The propylaea (Fig. V, 17) consists of a double colonnade. On the front of the first stood 10 columns. On both sides it had small prostyles with 6 columns each. Five doors (Fig. V, 18) behind this colonnade could be closed, isolating the temple from the rest of the sanctuary. (An inscription originating in this area regulated who could enter the temple, and under what conditions.) Part of the propylaea served as a sort of gallery (like the Dionysium in the ancient city of Rhodes); between the columns famous artists' paintings were hung and statues placed, whose bases survive to this day. The second, Doric, L-shaped stoa (Fig. V, 19) faced the inner courtyard and was made up of 17 columns. On one side of it were rooms (Fig. V, 20) which communicated internally and had doors on the inner courtyard (Fig. V, 21). Opposite it was an Ionic arcade (Fig. V, 23) from Roman times which abutted on the west wall of the temple – it is believed that Psithyrus, a prophet/demon in Aphrodite's entourage, was worshipped here; according to an inscription, he would not accept offerings of less than a drachma – and a wall with 6 columns (Fig. V, 22) which covered the rock, creating a peristyle inner courtyard. The novel arrangement of the propylaea complex and the stoa exerted an influence on the architecture of the Hellenistic Era in similar groups of buildings throughout Greece.

In the SE corner of one of the sanctuary's upper levels (116 m. above sea-level), in its SE corner, the small amphiprostyle (four columns on each end) Doric temple of Lindian Athena (Fig. V, 24) has been restored, so that it is visible from

View of the large, restored Hellenistic stoa (left) and the staircase (right)

all around. It is the oldest building on the acropolis, having stood there since the Archaic Era. The temple built by Cleobulus in the 6th century BC – which may have replaced an older one from the Geometric era – burned down in 392 BC, and the Classical temple was built on its foundation. At the end of the sekos, the spot (Fig. V, 26) can be distinguished on the rock where the cult statue stood. It is believed that in front of it there was a table (Fig. V, 25) where worshippers placed their offerings (gifts, fruit, etc.). As to the appearance of the Archaic statue, it is said to have represented Athena seated, with gold jewels around her neck and a golden wreath on her head. In the Classical-Age statue she was standing, holding a shield. One of the oldest statues of the goddess (600 BC) is said to have been made by Dipoenus and Skyles, sons of the mythical sculptor Daedalus. That work was burned in Constantinople, together with other "idolatrous" statues from Rhodes! The cult

of the goddess Lindia, thought to have been identified with Athena when the Dorians made their appearance, dates from the 9th century BC, but, as stated above, it is doubtful whether the temple existed at that time. The temple's refuse pit has yielded important examples of the miniature and plastic arts. On Mt. Krana (from the Doric word krini = fountain) opposite, the Archocratium can be seen.

Helios advised his sons to be the first to erect an altar on the acropolis of Lindus and to make sacrifices to the goddess Athena at the time of her birth, so as to win her favour (Homeric Hymn, Diodorus the Sicilian, Pindar). So, as Hephaestus hit Zeus' head with a bronze axe, and Athena sprang from it fully armed, the Heliades in their haste to make their sacrifice, forgot to light a fire. They conducted the sacrifice without fire (some archaeologists contend that this was the first fireless and bloodless sacrifice). Nevertheless Zeus, as Pindar informs us in his Ode, sent down a golden

The beginnings of the temple of Lindian Athena are lost in the mist of the centuries; it is the oldest building on the rock.

Remains of the large building in the northern annex of the proscenium of the theatre

rain which made Rhodes' fields fertile. The goddess became the protectress of the island and gave the Rhodians the gift of being foremost in the arts.

According to Diodorus the Sicilian (V, 58) the exiled King of Libya, Danaus – after a conspiracy against his brother, King Egyptus, or after an oracle prophesied that his brother would kill his 50 daughters – passed through Lindus on his way to Argos (1439 or 1510 BC). The inhabitants

The cavea of the ancient theatre, hollowed out of the rock below the acropolis

were so kind and attentive to him that he founded a sanctuary of Athena in Lindus, and erected a wooden statue of the goddess (which burned when the sanctuary caught fire), to thank her for having taught him to use sails on ships, as related by Apollodorus of Athens (II, 1, 4, 5-6). (The Danish archaeologists Kinch and Blinkenberg, in their study of the idol of Lindian Athena, maintain that, according to Mycenean customs and references by the Alexandrian poet Callimachus (310-240 BC), the goddess was represented by an unhewn chunk of wood or a plank with a smooth surface.) As to the renowned foundation of the Danaidae at the sanctuary, Pindar believed it was built by the Heliades, whereas Strabo believed it was built by Danaus himself (14, p. 655). One myth has it that the hero Tlepolemus named the three city-states of ancient Rhodes after the three daughters of Danaus, who died on the island.

Heretofore experts have believed that the sacrifices made at the temple were bloodless (seeds, honey-pies, etc.). In his History of the Ancient Rhodians (1900), Baron Hiller Van Gelder resorts to paroemiographers (such as Apostolius, XV, 25) to explain the phrase "Rhodian oracle". In order to sacrifice every day at the temple of Athena, the Rhodians remained night and day and even ate there. They asked Apollo if they could take with them the receptacle necessary for their bodily needs. Not satisfied that he gave his consent, they asked whether it should be of bronze or clay. The god would not condescend to answer them. The story became proverbial, for those who ask too many questions! But in fact the usually bloody animal sacrifices were practised on the altar outside the temple.

On the south slope of the acropolis hill, facing the small harbour, is the 4th-century BC ancient theatre, with a sitting capacity of over 1,800; its cavea has been hollowed out of the rock and its two ends built up. Here the Sminthia were celebrated, festivals dedicated to Dionysus, whose worship was widespread in the area. In the cavea above the diazoma there were 7 rows, and below it 19 rows of seats. Today 5 of the 9 blocks of seats remain, and the proedriae, the bottom row of seats for important personages, can be seen. Behind the circular orchestra, archaeologists have located the proscenium.

In the northern extension of the proscenium, note the fine workmanship on the stones of a large rectangular building of the 3rd-2nd century BC. Inside this building, which could hold 1,500-1,700 people, there was a four-sided Doric colonnade. Its proximity to the ancient theatre and the fact that it was later converted into a Christian place of worship – a common practice in Byzantine times – make it even more possible that it was originally built for religious purposes. Archaeologists believe that in early Byzantine times the building was converted into an early Christian basilica. Later, a Byzantine church was built on this spot, and after it was demolished by causes unknown, it was replaced by the smaller post-Byzantine Church of Agios Stefanos, which had to be torn down in the 1924 excavations. Around the church, early Christian and medieval tombs have been excavated.

Outstanding among the area's important finds are two very significant inscriptions, which had been used to pave the floor of the Byzantine church which formerly stood on the site of the Church of Agios Stefanos: they now repose, along with so many other Greek artefacts, in the Copenhagen museum. One of them is a *List of Priests* from 406 BC to 47 BC, inscribed on slabs of local grey marble which were located to the right and left of the temple entrance. The other is the *Chronicle of the Sanctuary* by the thc historian Timachidas, written on the recommendation of his father Agesitimus in 99 BC as a literary document. It was a record of the dedications to the temple from the age of myth (Cad-

The tomb of Cleobulus on Cape Agios Emilianos

mus, Minos, Heracles, Tlepolemus, Menelaus, Helen, etc.) up to the historical epoch (Cleobulus, Amasi, Artaphernes, Alexander the Great, Ptolemy, Pyrrus, etc.). The second part of the Chronicle tells of three epiphanies (epiphany = manifestation of a god to a mortal) of Athena (one when the Persian King Darius attacked Lindus, another when someone hanged himself in the temple and it had to be purified, and another when Rhodes was under siege by Demetrius the Besieger).

As concerns the introduction of the cult of Heracles to Lindus, Apollodorus the Athenian (II,5,11) and the paroemiographers Conon and Philostratus tell us how the phrase "Lindian sacrifice" came into being, in reference to a sacrifice performed disrespectfully and blasphemously. While travelling through Asia, Heracles put in at Thermydrus in Lindus and, because he was hungry, asked the first carter he met to slaughter one of the oxen pulling his cart. The carter explained to him that he needed

The Archocratium, as seen from the acropolis

the animal for his work. The irate Heracles slaughtered and ate both oxen, at the same time jeering at the poor carter, who rained down curses and imprecations on him the while. But the islanders admired Heracles' bravery and built an altar to him, which he called the "buzygon". There two oxen were to be sacrificed in memory of the ones he had eaten. Heracles made the carter priest of the temple, and ordered him always to accompany the sacrifice with imprecations, like the ones he had levelled at him, because he had never enjoyed a meal so much! If he accidentally uttered a good word, it was considered a desecration of the rite! It is said that the Lindians asked the famous artist Parrasius to paint them a picture featuring the hero.

Inscriptions on the inaccessible rocks north of the acropolis, on the side toward the open sea, identify this as the site of the Bucopion (= place where oxen are slaughtered). In the small 10th/9th-century BC temple which stood on the site, sacrifices were made in honour of some unknown god. In his excavations in the area in 1952, the archaeologist Dyggve found bronze statuettes.

On the side facing the big harbour, in the Vigli locale, a section of a mosaic attests to the existence of an early Christian basilica dating from the 5th or 6th century.

The area around the present-day settlement was an extensive cemetery, with graves from as far back as the Geometric Era. Of note are the two sepulchral monuments (mausoleums), the so-called "tomb of Cleobulus" and the "Archocratium". The first – the one visible from the acropolis, on a hillock on the peninsula opposite – is a small, sumptuous, circular building, perhaps from the Hellenistic Era, which probably belonged to a wealthy Lindian family. Made of carefully-hewn Lardos marble, it was converted into a church dedicated to Agios Emilianos in early Christian times. You can reach the building, vacant today, on foot or on donkey-back. The second,

hollowed out of the rock in the Kambana locale of Mt. Krana, is the large Hellenistic tomb of the Archocratus family. According to pre-1841 engravings, its ground-floor façade mimics a Doric stoa with a row of 12 columns that ended regularly in an epistyle, metopes and triglyphs and an imitation of decorative band of terra cotta tiles. The façade continued on the upper story with an equal number of columns and eleven blind openings between them. In front of them were four sepulchral altars, with the names of the dead on their bases; they can still be seen at its entrance. The interior consisted of a long, narrow corridor that ran off to the right and left of the tomb. A door separated it from the square room with tombs lining three of its sides. As it is also known as "Frangoklissia" ("Frankish church"), we may surmise that it was used as a Christian place of worship.

In the shadow of the imposing bare rock of the ancient acropolis, at the foot of Mt. Krana, is the traditional Aegean village of Lindos. It has been declared a protected monument, and the moment you enter it you will understand why. The great earthquake of 1610 brought about a building boom after 1620, but the village is built in an older style, since the only house to survive the quake dates from 1599 and is no different from the 17th-century houses. The Lindians, Rhodes' seafarers during the 15th and 16th centuries, were among the richest shipowners in the Aegean. Although their harbours were not particularly organised, they competed successfully with the organised European fleets. The main feature of town planning in that era, which became generalised in rural architecture in Rhodes, was the closing off of the narrow streets by high walls with no openings. The streets, thus isolated, prevented the indiscreet eyes of passers-by from peeking into courtyards or houses. The layout of the rooms and the decorated façades of ashgrey porous stone are modelled on the medieval architecture of Rhodes' Old Town.

The modern village of Lindos seems to have remained untouched from the time of the wealthy Lindian shipowners of the 15th century. Here you will forget the comforts of means of transport, as its narrow alleys are only big enough for people and donkeys.

A Rhodian plate with a peacock (from the book The Dodecanese *by Athina Tarsouli).*

The arched gate in the high wall leads into the pebble-paved courtyard. Usually a gatehouse of squared-off stones called the "pilionas" is built at the entrance to the

A neoclassical courtyard gate from the beginning of the 20th century

house. After the pilionas is the courtyard, paved with large brown or black and white pebbles implanted in a mortar containing sand and lime. The mosaics have themes taken from the ancient or Byzantine past, folk tradition or daily life.

Usually opposite the courtyard gate is the spacious room known as the "spitakla" or "sala", which functions as a reception area and usually occupies the whole width of the narrow building plot. Next to the door in a corner is a sheltered area for cooking and housework, together with an oven. A stone staircase leads to a small, low-ceilinged room – with windows on all sides, one of which, known as the "captain's room", is sure to have a view of the sea – above the pilionas. The separate low-ceilinged rooms on one or both free sides of the courtyard date from the second period of house-building in Lindos (late 17th-early 18th centuries).

The façade of the sala is the most heavily decorated part of the outside of the house: the jambs of its ogival door and window mouldings are decorated in carved braided or twisted-rope patterns and the space above the lintel contains rosettes, branches of plants, birds, etc. in bas-relief. This space often includes the year the house was built. To afford the room more light, apart from the decorated windows to the right and left of the door, three windows, also decorated, were added to the upper part of the façade (the middle one is smaller, ogival; the other two square).

The interior of the sala is divided in two by a tall, broad arch, necessary to support the ceiling, leaving a single, unencumbered space. The predilection for ornamentation is also apparent in the painted wooden ceiling and the pebble-mosaic floor of the sala. The plaster on the walls and the arch was also decorated with designs in intaglio or in relief. Lindian artistry reached its zenith in the Lindian plates ("skouteles"), which adorned the carved wooden shelves on the wall opposite the door, and in the hand-made cushions and the embroideries lining the shelves. Another fine piece of work in the traditional house was the "sperveri". It screened off the bed which stood on a raised platform in a corner of the room.

The decline of shipping during the 18th and 19th centuries forced many young people to emigrate. The remaining inhabitants limited themselves to the small rooms in the courtyard, and thus as time passed the old mansions fell into disrepair. The small white houses built since then look like humble rustic huts, compared to the magnificent captains' homes in the town, and make whitewash seem a shoddy material. Perceptible changes were brought about by the building of neoclassical houses or the conversion of the sea-captains' houses at the beginning of the 20th century. Houses now had large windows facing the street, their doors were decorated with parastades and classical lintels; they acquired a second story, their rooms communicated on the inside and they had peaked, terra cotta-tiled roofs.

Lindos will not deprive the visitor of the joy of discovery. You can wander through its winding lanes without fear of missing any of the sights. Ask one of the locals to show you the Papakonstandis mansion, built in 1622, which under the Italians became the country villa of the governor of the Archipelago, de Vecchi; today it is the property of the Archaeological Service. Other important old mansions are those of Moskouridi or Kira (1642) Theodoros (1643), Zoglos (17th century), Markoulitsa (17th century), Veatriki (1884), Makri (17th century), etc. But because most of them are closed, your only chance to see an interior may be in one that has been converted into a bar (and, like it or not, there are several of these latter).

The big parish Church of the Panagia was built ca. the 14th century on the site of

Tourist development in Lindos has not managed to alter its picturesque atmosphere. In the little shops you will find all kinds of souvenirs, in the restaurants you will sample all kinds of foods, and night falls with a promise of great things to come!

The parish church of Panagia, with important frescos, dating from the 18th century

The picturesque Church of Agios Georgios Hostos

an older church; it stood in the heart of the new settlement. Built into the small bell-tower at its entrance are the coats-of-arms of the Knight Jacques Aymer and Grand Master d'Aubusson. The latter donated the funds to repair its cruciform domed narthex in 1489, but the 20-meter-high neoclassical stone bell-tower was built later. The present-day appearance of the church and its outbuildings was formed in the neoclassical era. A lofty wall with an arched door stands between its pebble-paved courtyards and the street. The long, narrow church, in the form of a rough cross, houses exceptionally fine frescos painted in 1779 by Gregorius of Simi, in addition to portable icons and a carved and gilded wooden altar-screen dating from the 17th century. Its floor is paved with black and white bands of pebbles. The frescos in the northern chapel date from 1673-5. In a short time a small ecclesiastical museum will be set up in the house where the sexton lived.

In a small square in the southern part of Lindos stands the chapel of Agios Nikolaos. At some point your meanderings will take you to the cruciform domed Church of Agios Georgios Pahimahiotis, with frescos dating from 1393. It contains a painting of St. George on horseback, done by the folk artist of Simi, I. Spanos, in 1928. In a cave under the rock of the acropolis is the Church of Panagia Spiliotissa.

The indescribable beauty of the scene is completed by the vast azure sea which em-

Agios Nikolaos and Agios Georgios Pahimahiotis, lost among the congested buildings of Lindos

braces the rock, furnishing it with two natural harbours. Although there is no specific mention of it in the *Acts of the Apostles*, tradition has it that St. Paul landed in Lindos' small south harbour in AD 57, during his third voyage from Miletus in Asia Minor to Syria. In 1951, as part of the worldwide commemoration of St. Paul's journeys, the little chapel of Agii Apostoli was built. Every year a festival is held here on June 29.

In Lindos many small single-aisled churches with frescos have survived from the 11th, 12th and 13th centuries. On the slope facing the large harbour stands the Church of Agios Sotirios; near the village centre are the Churches of Agios Georgios, Mihail Stratilatis, the basilica of Agios Dimitrios, the cruciform domed Church of Agios Minas, with an altar supported by an ancient marble column capital or statue, and frescos painted in the 12th and 15th centuries. Finally, there is the underground Church of Agios Georgios Hostos, whose frescos date from the 8th or 9th and 12th centuries; it is built in a form of the Greek

The harbour of St. Paul with the chapel of the Apostles

cross. In the village cemetery the Church of Faneromeni was built in 1932.

In the large harbour, next to the natural caves in the cliff which were formerly used as storehouses, a few small homes were built late in the 19th century. Today, the little beach fills up with bamboo umbrellas and bathers enjoying the superb sea. Further on along the same bay stretches the fine organised beach of Lindos, where you can engage in your favourite sports.

The fine organised beach in Lindos' big harbour

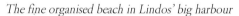

Frequented beaches and isolated inlets make up the Bay of Lardos.

Don't be fooled by the apparent calm in this lovely bay in Kiotari. It is only a few minutes after sunrise.

Rhodes – Apolakia – Katavia – Prassonissi

Our next itinerary includes the rest of the villages in what was the ancient city-state of Lindia.

The road that runs along the coast beyond Lindos passes the charming little beaches on Lardos Bay (Plakia, Makris Tihos, Lothiarika, Glistra), which are hard to resist. If you continue on, you will be re-warded by the traditional villages in the south. In the newly-built tourist resort of **Kiotari**, with several luxury hotels, rooms to rent and restaurants, you will find the island's only shooting range with moving targets. At the Eftavimati site stands a single-aisled 4th/5th-century basilica.

Turning right off the coastal road you pass the Monastery of the Transfiguration, which celebrates its saint's day on August 6. Further on is the traditional village of

The church of the Dormition of the Virgin, built in 1080, with 17th-century frescos, in Asklipio.

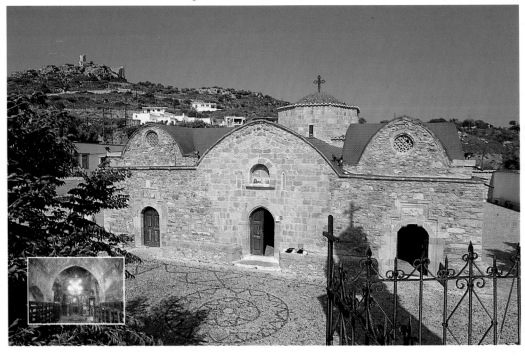

The agrarian section of the Asklipio museum

The Byzantine fortress of Asklipio

Asklipio, which has been declared a protected architectural monument; it took its name from the Aesculapium which once existed there. In the roughly cruciform Byzantine Church of the Dormition of the Virgin, with a dome and 17th-century frescos, built in 1060 over the ruins of an early Christian church, a traditional saint's-day festival is held on August 15. Behind the church is a building dating from 1906 which houses a folklore museum, consisting of an ecclesiastical and an agrarian section (opening hours 10:00 am-5:00 pm daily). In the ecclesiastical section, fine icons, manuscript gospels dating from 1540, priests' vestments and other liturgical objects are on display. In the agrarian section, the exhibits include household utensils, farming tools and equipment (an old mechanical oil-press, an oil filter and an oil still). A footpath leads to a rocky height next to the village, site of the Byzantine fortress of Asklipio, seat of the area's feudal lord. Above the main gate,

The organised beach at Genadi

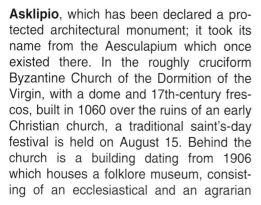

The Church of Agios Ioannis, built in 1924, at Vati.

The interior of a traditional house (above) and the Church of Agios Georgios in Profilia (below).

the emblem of the Pope is built into the wall. Fallen masonry and the thick brushy vegetation make it difficult of access, but soon it will be visitable. Only two of its towers are standing, one on the SE corner, restored in 1935, and the other on the NW corner.

On the right side of the main road is touristy **Genadi**, with plenty of rooms to rent, typical Rhodian vacation homes, and the Church of Agios Ioannis. The village took its name from a landowner named Genadis. The Church of Agia Anastassia Romea in the cemetery incorporates architectural members taken from the early Christian basilica it replaced. Between here and Plimiri are a string of sandy inlets, ideal for a solitary dip. On the road to Lahania is the old Monastery of Agios Ioannis, which holds its saint's-day celebrations on May 5.

The road now turns inland; following it you will discover that Rhodes' beauties are not restricted to its seaside areas. In traditional **Vati** you can have a cup of coffee in the quaint coffee-house in the shade of the venerable plane-tree in the square. The village has two churches: the older, of Agios Ioannis, dates from 1924, and the newer white Church of Agios Savas, on the hilltop, from 1969. On another hill stand the ruins of a mill demolished when the Italians bombed it. In this area, plundered Mycenean tombs and two Geometric tombs containing pottery and gold coins have been excavated. Be patient as you drive through the depressing burnt forests, because the picturesque mountain village of **Profilia** awaits you. Ancient Istros, which took its modern name from the outpost once located here, was in this area. The church dedicated to the Nativity of the Virgin celebrates its saint's day in the traditional way on September 8. But what you must have the exceptionally hospitable villagers show you is the stone chapel of Agios Georgios, formerly of the Taxiarhis, with splendid frescos dating from 1017. As you admire the view to the south of the village, you will notice that the roofs of the older houses are made of patelia (earth, oil and salt mixture). The village's traditional houses consist of a single room divided in two by an arch. Decorative plates adorn the walls, and hand embroidered pieces cover the furniture.

The road runs down to the old village of **Istrios**, boasting flowering gardens and the Church of Agios Merkourios. It may have taken its name from the fact that its inhabitants migrated there from nearby ("paristries") territories.

In the village of **Apolakia**, the houses are whitewashed and have terra cotta-tiled roofs. In addition to the quaint tavernas in the square, see the old Church of Agios Georgios, the newer one of Agia Marina, which celebrates its saint's day on July 17, and the Monastery of Assomati. Near Agia Marina the foundations and walls of a Crusader castle can be seen. Excavations in 1904 revealed plundered Mycenean tombs

The Church of Agios Merkourios in Istrios

at the Mili site, and Hellenistic tombs at the Korkoelia site. Near Apolakia dam is the single-aisled basilica of Agios Georgios Vardas with important Byzantine frescos dating from 1289/90. On the road to Katavia, at the Peli site, architectural members of an early Christian church dedicated to Agia Anastassia were recently discovered; nearby is a cemetery from the same era. On the way to Arnitha, hidden in a fenced-in field among broad-leaved fig-

The basilica of Agios Georgios Vardas, near Apolakia

trees, is the mosaic floor of the Byzantine basilica of Agia Irini (you will have difficulty finding it, and cannot get close to it anyway). Its baptismal font has been made into a fountain which now adorns Argirokastro Square in the Old Town. Next is the old village of **Arnitha**, where you can relax in the square shaded by plane and eucalyptus trees, where Nikolaos Plastiras sat in 1933 in exile and again in 1950 as Prime Minister of Greece. The Monastery of Agios Filimonas – a saint who cured the insane –, with an early Christian conventual church, holds religious festivities twice a year, on July 21 and November 22. On Paleokastro hill, traces of a small settlement, a castle and Hellenistic tombs were discovered in 1904.

Because the road from Arnitha to Messanagros is unpaved, those not driving a 4X4 vehicle would be well advised to return to the coast road and drive to Messanagros via Lahania. (On the dirt road, you will see the ruins of the Church of Agia Varvara.)

In **Lahania**, which boasts a hotel and a few rooms to rent in homes, see the village square with the fountains, the old Italian wash-houses and the mills which once ground the wheat for this area. Next to the Monastery of Agios Georgios, the ruins of a small Mycenean fortress were excavated in 1905. Also worth visiting are the Monasteries of Agia Irini, Agios Loukas and Profitis Ilias on a hill outside the village. On the waterfront, the foundations of a church dedicated to Agios Avakoum have been fenced off. On the road to Messanagros, visit the Monasteries of the Saviour and of Agios Thomas, with important 15th-century frescos. The last little whitewashed stone church, housing well-preserved frescos, has picnic tables in its courtyard for visitors who have brought their lunch with them.

In the old mountain village of **Messanagros** – which was named thus because it

The Church of Agia Irini in Lahania

Above: *The Church of Agios Filimonas in Arnitha*

Below: *The stone chapel of Agios Thomas*

is surrounded by fields ("messi" = middle; "agros" = field), the main church is dedicated to the Taxiarhis. But your attention will be drawn to the Church of the Dormition, dating from the 16th-17th centuries. It was built in the middle of a big 5th-century early Christian basilica. To the latter belong the two columns with capitals, the mosaic floor, the few remaining frescos, and the white marble baptismal font, decorated in bas-relief. Two kilometres outside the village, on a level patch of ground on Mt. Skiadi, stands the monastery of the same name. On the top of the mountain (elevation approx. 600 m.), commanding a marvellous view, stands a wooden cross. A folk tradition connected with this monastery has it that the rocky islet of Htenia opposite was once a pirate ship (and admittedly it does resemble one), but was turned to stone by the Virgin Mary as the pirates

prepared to attack the monastery!

Because Messanagros is linked to Katavia by an unpaved road, you may return to Lahania and continue on towards the Bay of **Plimiri** (= bay with currents, where the water rises and falls with the tides), with dark-coloured sand and two small tavernas. Inside the conventual church of the small Monastery of Zoodohos Pigi, built in 1840 over the ruins of an early Christian basilica, notice the column drums and Corinthian capitals incorporated in the walls, as well as the carvings on the altar-screen and pulpit. First to contend that there had been an ancient city on this site were the archaeologists Billioti and Salzmann (1852-1864). In 1902-1905 the base of a marble basin and Hellenistic tombs were found. According to tradition, the village received its name from the crowds of pilgrims who inundated its narthex ("plimi-

Left: The Church of the Dormition of the Virgin in Messanagros. Older architectural members were used to build it.
Right: The Monastery of Panagia Skiadeni at sunset

The Church of Zoodohos Pigi in Plimiri

ra" = flood), to obtain a little miraculous holy water. Continue on towards the ghost-village of **Agios Pavlos**, which has been abandoned since 1948. It begs to be photographed, with fields of wheat in the foreground, and behind them the old Catholic Church of San Paolo and the ruined houses of the Italian colonists. The road ends in the tourist resort of **Katavia** (ancient Cattabus), which offers rooms to rent, tavernas and bars. In the village cemetery, see the old cruciform Church of the Dormition of the Virgin, with fine 17th-century frescos and marble parts of an early Christian basilica built into its walls. Between 1905 and 1915, excavations were carried out in this area on Mycenean and Hellenistic tombs. Near the Church of Agios Pandeleimon a necropolis with tombs dating from 550 BC has been excavated.

As a fitting culmination to your visit to the island, you may want to view a unique spectacle. A passable dirt road (but as busy as a motorway!) 11 km. from Katavia

The enchanting picture presented by the itinerary into the southern part of Rhodes

The Church of the Dormition of the Virgin (left) in Katavia cemetery, and a quaint coffee-shop in the village (right)

will take you to an other-worldly scene. A broad sandy peninsula about 2 km. long connects the coast with the rocky islet of **Prassonissi**. In the two vast bays formed here, hundreds of swimmers and surfers enjoy the crystal-clear waters (swimmers on the left and surfers in the place of honour on the right!) Anyone lucky enough to find a table will enjoy a meal at one of the two little tavernas, which are flooded in the winter when the water level rises. On the islet is a beacon for passing ships.

At the Frodia (Prassou) site, traces of a temple were unearthed in 1905, with a precinct wall and an altar. Early in the 20th century, Danish archaeologists discovered the seaside settlement of Brulia, dating from the end of the Geometric and beginning of the Archaic period, where the well-known 6th-century BC pottery was found.

On Rhodes' isolated southern tip, cut off in winter from the rest of the island, Prassonissi makes a picture of rare beauty.

Bibliography

Αρχαία Ρόδος, «2400 χρόνια», Ministry of Culture, 22nd Ephorate of Prehistoric and Classical Antiquities of the Dodecanese, Athens 1993

Auberge de France à Rhodes, Institut Français d'Athènes, 1986

Δωδεκανησιακά Χρονικά, Volume II, Στέγη γραμμάτων και τεχνών Δωδεκανήσου, Athens 1974

Δωδεκανησιακά Χρονικά, Volume III, Στέγη γραμμάτων και τεχνών Δωδεκανήσου, Athens 1977

Δωδεκανησιακά Χρονικά, Volume VI, Στέγη γραμμάτων και τεχνών Δωδεκανήσου, Athens 1979

Δωδεκανησιακά Χρονικά, Volume IX, Στέγη γραμμάτων και τεχνών Δωδεκανήσου, Athens 1983

Δωδεκανησιακά Χρονικά, Volume X, Στέγη γραμμάτων και τεχνών Δωδεκανήσου, Athens 1984

Δωδεκανησιακά Χρονικά, Volume IXI, Στέγη γραμμάτων και τεχνών Δωδεκανήσου, Athens 1986

Δωδεκανησιακά Χρονικά, Volume XII, Στέγη γραμμάτων και τεχνών Δωδεκανήσου, Athens 1987

Μουσεία της Ρόδου II, «Πινακοθήκη, Μουσείο Λαϊκής Τέχνης, Καστέλλο», Editions Απόλλων

Πάπυρος Λαρούς Μπριτάννικα, Editions Πάπυρος, 1992

Πολιτιστικά Δωδεκανήσου, «Εισηγήσεις και πορίσματα του Α΄ πολιτιστικού συμποσίου Δωδεκανήσου '78», Στέγη Γραμμάτων & Τεχνών Δωδεκανήσου, series of independent publications, No. 11, Athens 1981

Rhodes, «Olympic color», Athens

Ρόδος, «Ιαλυσός – Κάμιρος – Λίνδος – και το μουσείο της Ρόδου», Editions Κλειώ, 1977

Ημερολόγιον 1994, Holy Monastery of the Archangel Michael Thari, Holy Metropolis of Rhodes

The complete traveller's guide to Rodos, «Sightseeing-Hotels-Practical Information», Tourist Publications, Athens 1985

NIKOS ALEXIS: *Ρόδος*, Π. Ευσταθιάδης & Υιοί Α. Ε., Athens 1985

MICHAEL E. ARFARAS: *Τα αρχοντικά της Λίνδου και η λαογραφία τους*, Athens 1976

BAUD-BOVY S.: *Τραγούδια των Δωδεκανήσων*, Volume I & II, Association for the Dissemination of Useful Books, Municipality of Rhodes Cultural Organisation

CHR. GIOVANIS: *Μεγάλη εγκυκλοπαίδεια*, Editions Χ. Γιοβάνη, 1978

CHRISTOS I. KAROUZOS: *Ρόδος*, «Ιστορία – Μνημεία – Τέχνη», Athens 1949

ILIAS KOLIAS: *Η μεσαιωνική πόλη της Ρόδου και το παλάτι του Μεγάλου Μαγίστρου*, Ministry of Culture - Archaeological Resources Fund, Athens 1994

ILIAS KOLIAS: *Ιππότες της Ρόδου*, «Το παλάτι και η πόλη», Ekdotike Athenon S.A., Athens 1991

K.N. KONSTANTINIDIS: *Αθανά Λίνδια*, Alexandria 1936

GRIGORIS KONSTANTINOPOULOS: *Αρχαία Ρόδος*, «Επισκόπηση της ιστορίας και της τέχνης», National Bank of Greece Educational Institute, Athens 1986

GRIGORIS KONSTANTINOPOULOS: *Λίνδος*, Editions Απόλλων

GRIGORIS KONSTANTINOPOULOS: *Ιαλυσός – Κάμιρος*, Editions Απόλλων

MICHALAKI-KOLLIA MARIA: *All Rhodes*, Editorial Escudo de Oro S. A. & Ghinis Trading and Publishing LTD., Athens 1987

EDOUARD BILIOTTI - ABBA COTTRET: *Η νήσος Ρόδος*, 1881

THEOFANIS BOGIANNOS: *Ρόδος*, «240 συναπτές δεκαετίες ακραιφνούς ελληνισμού»

ANASTASSIOS K. ORLANDOS: *Αρχείον των βυζαντινών μνημείων της Ελλάδος*, Volume III, No. 1, Athens 1948

MANOLIS D. PAPAIOANNOU: *Ρόδος και Αρχαία κείμενα*, Editions Δωδώνη, Athens-Gianena 1986

MANOLIS D. PAPAIOANNOU: *Διαγόρας Ολυμπιονίκης ο Ρόδιος*, Diagoras Gymnastic Club, Athens 1983

C. PAPAHRISTODOULOU: *Ιστορία της Ρόδου*, «Από τους προϊστορικούς χρόνους έως την ενσωμάτωση της Δωδεκανήσου (1948)», Athens 1972

PETROCHEILOU ANNA: *The Greek caves*, Ekdotike Athenon S. A., Athens 1984

PINDAR: *Ολυμπία*, Είδος Ζ΄ ςίχ. 100-140

JEAN RISPEN: *Μεγάλη Ελληνική Μυθολογία*, Volume I & II, Editions Π. Κουτσούμπος, Athens 1949

144

STRABO: Γεωγραφικά, ιδ΄ 2, 7

SORENSEN WRIEDT LONE – PENTZ PETER: Lindos IV, 2, «Excavations and Surveys in Southern Rhodes: The Post-Mycenean Periods until Roman Times and the Medieval Period», The National Museum of Denmark, Copenhagen 1992

ATHINA TARSOULI: Δωδεκάνησα, Volume I, Editions Άλφα, Athens 1947

ARGIRO V. TATAKI: Ρόδος, «Λίνδος – Κάμιρος – Φιλέρημος. Το παλάτι των Μεγάλων Μαγίστρων», Ekdotike Athenon S.A., Athens 1988

ARGIRO V. TATAKI: Lindos, «The Acropolis and the medieval castle», Ekdotike Athenon S. A., Athens 1986

ΦΙΝΑ ΚΥΡΙΑΚΟΥ Ι.: Ρόδος, «2400 χρόνια (408 π. Χ.-1992 μ. Χ.)», a publication of the Dodecanese Chamber of Commerce and Industry, Rhodes 1992

KIRIAKOS I. FINAS: Η παιδεία στη Λίνδο στα χρόνια της σκλαβιάς, «(Τουρκοκρατία – Ιταλοκρατία) 1522-1945», 1991

KIRIAKOS I. FINAS: Η Δωδεκανησιακή οικονομία από της απελευθερώσεως της Δωδεκανήσου μέχρι σήμερα 1947-1989, «Προϋφισταμένη κατάσταση – Μεταπελευθερωτικές εξελίξεις – Προβλήματα και προοπτικές», a publication of the Dodecanese Chamber of Commerce and Industry, 1991

IOANNA FOKA, PANOS VALAVANIS: Ανακαλύπτω την Αρχαία Ελλάδα, «Αρχιτεκτονική και Πολεοδομία», Editions Κέδρος, Athens 1992

How to Get There

• You can sail to Rhodes on one of the frequent car and passenger ferries from Piraeus (tel. 4135 716/4135 730), stopping at some or all of the following ports: Kos, Patmos, Leros, Kalimnos, Paros, Amorgos, Astipalea, Nissiros, Tilos, Simi, Kastelorizo, Halki, Kassos, Karpathos, Crete, Ikaria, Samos, Hios, Lesvos, Limnos, Kavala. The local Dodecanese line connects Rhodes with several islands (Simi, Tilos, Nissiros, Kos, Kastelorizo, Lipsi, Patmos, Agathonissi, Samos, Halki, Karpathos). In summer sailings are more frequent and routes change according to needs at any given time.
• In the summertime, Flying Dolphin hydrofoils link Rhodes with various other Aegean islands.
• Travel agents organise excursions on the caiques that ply from Mandraki to various seaside spots.
• Olympic Airways has flights from Rhodes' airport at Paradissi to Hellenicon Airport in Athens (9666 666) daily, and to other Greek airports on certain days of the week (Thessaloniki, Kassos, Mytilene, Kastelorizo, Karpathos, Kos, Sitia, Iraklio) or only in summer (Santorini, Paros, Mykonos). There are also connections with the principal cities of Western Europe.

Useful Phone Numbers

Rhodes area code	0241
Municipality	35074/25515/25521/25533
Police	100/33333
E.O.T. (National Tourist Organisation)	23655/23355/27466
Tourist Police	27423
Rhodes First Aid Station	166/25580
Red Cross Hospital	22222/25555
Pharmacy	22559
List of pharmacies open nights or weekends	107
Central Harbour Master's Office	22220/22203/28666
Mandraki Port Authority	27695
Mandraki	23693
Steamer and hydrofoil ships' agent	20666
Inter-city bus office	27706
Local bus station	24129
Taxi stand	64712/64734/64756
Olympic Airways on Rhodes	24571-5
Paradissi Airport	91771
Palace of the Grand Masters	23359

Archaeological Museum			27657
Museum of Traditional Decorative Arts			34719
Aquarium			25936
Municipal Picture Gallery			23766
Municipal Library			21954/37144
Filerimos (Ialissos' Acropolis)			92202
Ancient Kamiros			41435

(The above numbers have been taken from the 1994 Rhodes Business Directory*)*

List of Hotels

GRAND HOTEL ASTIR PALACE•	Rhodes	AA	26284
ATHINEON ••	Rhodes	A	26112
BELVEDERE•	Rhodes	A	24471
BLUE SKY•	Rhodes	A	24091
CHEVALIERS PALACE•	Rhodes	A	22781
ESAIAS ••	Rhodes	A	22357/29263
EVA ••	Rhodes	A	29508
GOLDEN SUN ••	Rhodes	A	63983/63897
HELIOS ••	Rhodes	A	30033
IBISCUS•	Rhodes	A	24421
IMPERIAL•	Rhodes	A	22431
KAMIROS•	Rhodes	A	22591
MEDITERRANEAN•	Rhodes	A	24661
MIRAGE ••	Rhodes	A	37417
NIKOS-TINA•••	Rhodes	A	21060
REGINA•	Rhodes	A	22171
RIVIERA•	Rhodes	A	22581/24801
SIRAVAST•	Rhodes	A	23551
SIRENE BEACH•	Rhodes	A	30650/23765
STEVY ••	Rhodes	A	37003
VERINO•	Rhodes	A	34881/22625
ACANDIA•	Rhodes	B	22251
AGLAIA•	Rhodes	B	22061
ALEXANDROS ••	Rhodes	B	34196
ALEXIA•	Rhodes	B	24061
AMPHITRYON•	Rhodes	B	26880
ANGELA•	Rhodes	B	24614
AQUARIUS•	Rhodes	B	28107
ATHINA•	Rhodes	B	22631
BEACH HOTEL 33•	Rhodes	B	23857
BELLA VISTA•	Rhodes	B	29900
CACTUS•	Rhodes	B	26100
CAPITOL•••	Rhodes	B	74154
CASA ANTICA•••	Rhodes	B	26206
CAVO D'ORO•••	Rhodes	B	36980
CITY CENTER•	Rhodes	B	36612
CONSTANTIN•	Rhodes	B	22971
CONTINENTAL•	Rhodes	B	30885
CORALLI•	Rhodes	B	24912
DESPO•	Rhodes	B	22571
EMMANUEL•	Rhodes	B	22892/36010
ERODIA ••	Rhodes	B	31361/34741
ESPERIA•	Rhodes	B	23941
EUROPA•	Rhodes	B	22902/24810
GEORGE ••	Rhodes	B	21964
INTEUROPA ••	Rhodes	B	30642
LEFKA ••	Rhodes	B	34959/36792
LOMENIZ•	Rhodes	B	35748/35770-7

146

LOTUS•	Rhodes	B	21653
MANOUSOS•	Rhodes	B	22741
OLYMPIC•	Rhodes	B	24311
PALM•	Rhodes	B	24531
PANORAMA ••	Rhodes	B	37800
PLAZA•	Rhodes	B	22501
PRINCESS FLORA•	Rhodes	B	62010
SPARTALIS•	Rhodes	B	24371
SANDY COAST ••	Rhodes	B	22240
STELLA•••	Rhodes	B	24935
SUNRISE ••	Rhodes	B	30009
THERMAI•	Rhodes	B	24351
ACHILLION•	Rhodes	C	24604/22391
ADONIS•	Rhodes	C	27791
AEGAION•	Rhodes	C	22491
AEGLI•	Rhodes	C	22789
AFRICA•	Rhodes	C	24979/24645
ALS•	Rhodes	C	22481
AMARYLLIS•	Rhodes	C	24522
AMBASSANDER•	Rhodes	C	24679
ASTRON•	Rhodes	C	24651
ATLANTIS•	Rhodes	C	24821
BUTTERFLY•	Rhodes	C	24207
CARINA•	Rhodes	C	22381
CONGO•	Rhodes	C	24023/24029
DIANA•	Rhodes	C	24677
EL GRECO•	Rhodes	C	24071
ELIT•	Rhodes	C	22391
EMBONA•	Rhodes	C	24139
EMERALD ••	Rhodes	C	34322
ERO ••	Rhodes	C	31724
FEDRA•	Rhodes	C	22791
FLORA•	Rhodes	C	24538/26130
FLORIDA•	Rhodes	C	22111
FOUR SEASONS•	Rhodes	C	22340
HELENA•	Rhodes	C	24755
HERMES•	Rhodes	C	26022/27677
IMPALA ••	Rhodes	C	36856/29704
INTERNATIONAL•	Rhodes	C	24595
ISABELLA•	Rhodes	C	22651
KAPPA STUDIOS•	Rhodes	C	36841
KYPRIOTIS•	Rhodes	C	35921
LYDIA•	Rhodes	C	22705/22871/24707
MAJESTIC•	Rhodes	C	22031
MANISKAS ••	Rhodes	C	37412
MARIE•	Rhodes	C	30577
MARIETTE •••	Rhodes	C	34593
MIMOZA•	Rhodes	C	24026/20432
MINOS•	Rhodes	C	24041
MOSCHOS•	Rhodes	C	24764
NAFSIKA•	Rhodes	C	73040-1
NEW YORK•	Rhodes	C	22841
NOUΓANA	Rhodes	C	24545
ORION •••	Rhodes	C	35338
PARTHENON•	Rhodes	C	22351
PAVLIDES•	Rhodes	C	20281
PEARL•	Rhodes	C	22420-1
PHILOXENIA•	Rhodes	C	37244
RAINBOW•	Rhodes	C	75506-7/73306-11
ROYAL•	Rhodes	C	24601

SARONIS•	Rhodes	C	22811
SAVOY•	Rhodes	C	20721
SEMIRAMIS•	Rhodes	C	20741
ST. ANTONIO•	Rhodes	C	24971
SUNNY ••	Rhodes	C	33030
SYLVIA•	Rhodes	C	22551
TILOS•	Rhodes	C	24591
VASSILIA•	Rhodes	C	35239/24051
VENUS•	Rhodes	C	29990/24668
VICTORIA•	Rhodes	C	24626
VILLA RODOS•	Rhodes	C	20614
ANASTASIA•	Rhodes	D	21815
ANNA MARIA•	Rhodes	D	73685
ARIETTE•	Rhodes	D	22490
ATLAS•	Rhodes	D	35944
DORIAN ••	Rhodes	D	31756
EFROSYNI•	Rhodes	D	73222
EVELYN•	Rhodes	D	73720
KAHLUA•	Rhodes	D	33357
MANOS•	Rhodes	D	22620
PANTHEON•	Rhodes	D	24557
PARIS•	Rhodes	D	26356
RODIAKON•	Rhodes	D	22051-2
RODINI•	Rhodes	D	27814
SEVA S ••	Rhodes	D	26213
SEVEN PALMS ••	Rhodes	D	36830
SOLARIS•	Rhodes	D	30611/24420
STAR•	Rhodes	D	22853
XANTHI•	Rhodes	D	24996
ZEPHYROS•	Rhodes	D	22826
ARIS•	Rhodes	E	23312
ATTALIA•	Rhodes	E	23595
ATTIKI•	Rhodes	E	27767
ATHINEA•	Rhodes	E	23221
DORA•	Rhodes	E	24523
ILIANA•	Rhodes	E	30251
KASTRO•	Rhodes	E	20446
KRITI•	Rhodes	E	21341
LA LUNA•	Rhodes	E	25876/25856
LIA•	Rhodes	E	26209
MARGET•	Rhodes	E	31938/25289
MASSARI•	Rhodes	E	22469
NEW VILLAGE INN•	Rhodes	E	34937
OLD CITY•	Rhodes	E	36951
PICADILLY•	Rhodes	E	61937
SO NICOL•	Rhodes	E	34561
SPOT•	Rhodes	E	34737
STASA•	Rhodes	E	28279
STATHIS•	Rhodes	E	24357
SYDNEY•	Rhodes	E	25965
CYMI•	Rhodes	E	23917
TEHERANI•	Rhodes	E	27594
ZEUS•	Rhodes	E	23129
CATHRIN•••••.	Ladiko	A	85080
LADIKO••••••	Ladiko	A	85636
ESPEROS VILLAGE••••••	Faliraki	AA	86046
APOLLO BEACH•	Faliraki	A	85535
BLUE SEA•	Faliraki	A	85582/85512

CALYPSO•	Faliraki	A	85455
CALYPSO PALACE•	Faliraki	A	85621
COLOSSOS BEACH•	Faliraki	A	85524/85502
COLUMBIA RESORT •••••	Faliraki	A	85610
DANAE•••	Faliraki	A	85969
EPSILON ••	Faliraki	A	85269/85956
ESPERIDES•	Faliraki	A	85178/271/267/912
ESPEROS PALACE•	Faliraki	A	85734
FALIRAKI BEACH•	Faliraki	A	85301
OLYMPOS BEACH•	Faliraki	A	85490/87511-2
PEGASSOS BEACH•	Faliraki	A	85103
RODOS BEACH•	Faliraki	A	85412/85471
SUN PALACE•	Faliraki	A	85650
ACHOUSA•	Faliraki	B	85970
ATALANTI•	Faliraki	B	85255
BLUE STAR•••••.	Faliraki	B	85533
ERATO•	Faliraki	B	85414
IRINA ••	Faliraki	B	86070
MODUL•	Faliraki	B	85548
MOUSSES•	Faliraki	B	85303/85625
VIOLETTA ••	Faliraki	B	85501
ALOE•	Faliraki	C	86146
ANASTA ••	Faliraki	C	85311
ARGO•	Faliraki	C	85461
DIAMANTIS ••	Faliraki	C	85236/85235
DIMITRA•	Faliraki	C	85309
EDELWEISS•	Faliraki	C	85442/85305
EVI•	Faliraki	C	85586
FALIRAKI BAY•	Faliraki	C	85645
GONDOLA•	Faliraki	C	85759
HERCULES•	Faliraki	C	85002
IDEAL•	Faliraki	C	85518
KOSTAS ••	Faliraki	C	85520
LIDO•	Faliraki	C	85226
LYMBERIA•	Faliraki	C	85676
MARAN•	Faliraki	C	86108/85913
MATINA•	Faliraki	C	85835
NATASA ••	Faliraki	C	85507
RODANIA ••	Faliraki	C	85421/85614
SEA VIEW•	Faliraki	C	85903/85925
SEMELI ••	Faliraki	C	85247
SOFIA•	Faliraki	C	85423
STAMATIA •••	Faliraki	C	85263
TELCHINES•	Faliraki	C	85003/85025
TIVOLI•	Faliraki	C	86020
TSAMBIKA•	Faliraki	C	85760
VENETIA•	Faliraki	C	85612
K. SOTRILLIS ••	Faliraki	D	86070
PLATON•	Faliraki	D	85229/85592
SALIS•	Faliraki	D	85006
ANTONIOS•	Faliraki	E	85100
CAMBANA•	Faliraki	E	85281/85543
CHRYSOULA•	Faliraki	E	85660
DAFNI•	Faliraki	E	85544
FALIRO•	Faliraki	E	85399
FIESTA•	Faliraki	E	85498
IKAROS•	Faliraki	E	85242
MARIANNA•	Faliraki	E	85238
NEFELI•	Faliraki	E	85658
NEST•	Faliraki	E	85390/85581

ODYSSIA•	Faliraki	E	85288
PLATANOS•	Faliraki	E	85570
REA•	Faliraki	E	85221
RENA•	Faliraki	E	85120/22801
ST. AMON•	Faliraki	E	85430
STAMOS•	Faliraki	E	85643
STEVE•	Faliraki	E	85293
SYNTHIA•	Faliraki	E	85298
FALIRAKI•••••••	Faliraki		85516/85338
GRECOTEL RHODOS IMPERIAL•	Ialissos	AA	75000
MIRA MARE BEACH•••••.	Ialissos	AA	96251
OLYMPIC PALACE•	Ialissos	AA	28755
RODOS PALACE•••••.	Ialissos	AA	25222
ANITA •••	Ialissos	A	94258
APOLLONIA ••	Ialissos	A	92951
AVRA BEACH•	Ialissos	A	25284
BEL AIR•	Ialissos	A	23731
BENELUX ••	Ialissos	A	93716
BLUE BAY•••••.	Ialissos	A	91137/91131-2
BLUE HORIZON•	Ialissos	A	93481-4
CARAVEL ••	Ialissos	A	96843
COSMOPOLITAN•••••.	Ialissos	A	35373
DIONYSOS•	Ialissos	A	23021
EDEM•••	Ialissos	A	94284/94044
ELECTRA PALACE•	Ialissos	A	92521
ELINA•	Ialissos	A	92466/92944
ELIZABETH ••	Ialissos	A	92656
FILERIMOS ••	Ialissos	A	92510/92933
FILERIMOS•••••.	Ialissos	A	92510/92933
GOLDEN BEACH No 1 &2 •	Ialissos	A	92411
IALYSOS BAY•	Ialissos	A	91841
LATIN BEACH ••	Ialissos	A	94053
MARIBEL ••	Ialissos	A	94001
METROPOLITAN CAPSIS•	Ialissos	A	25015
OCEANIS•	Ialissos	A	24881
OSIRIS ••	Ialissos	A	94717
PALEOS ••	Ialissos	A	92431
POSEIDONIA•	Ialissos	A	22276
RODOS BAY•	Ialissos	A	23661
SEA MELODY ••	Ialissos	A	91026
SUN BEACH No 1 & No 2••	Ialissos	A	93821
SUNNY DAYS ••	Ialissos	A	90006/96961
ALIA ••	Ialissos	B	31410
ALKYON ••	Ialissos	B	28637
ANIXIS ••	Ialissos	B	91857
ARGO SEA ••	Ialissos	B	90163
COSMOS ••	Ialissos	B	94080
ELEONAS ••	Ialissos	B	91376/94602
FORUM ••	Ialissos	B	94321
GALINI ••	Ialissos	B	94406
KASSANDRA ••	Ialissos	B	94236
LE COCOTIERS•	Ialissos	B	96450
LITO•	Ialissos	B	23511
LIZA•••	Ialissos	B	93557
MARITINA ••	Ialissos	B	96955/90954
MATOULA BEACH•	Ialissos	B	94251/93264
NIKI •••	Ialissos	B	94065/92064
PACHOS ••	Ialissos	B	92514/22328
SOLEMAR•	Ialissos	B	96941

SUMMERLAND•••••.	Ialissos	B	94941
SWAN ••	Ialissos	B	94502
WING ••	Ialissos	B	96361
BELLE ELENE•	Ialissos	B	92173
IALYSOS CITY•	Ialissos	B	93162
ARLEKINO ••	Ialissos	C	94255
BLUE EYES ••	Ialissos	C	36797
DEBBY ••	Ialissos	C	94651
EL DORADO ••	Ialissos	C	94021-2
ELENI•	Ialissos	C	93717
GREEN VIEW•	Ialissos	C	91009
IXIA ••	Ialissos	C	29988
MICHAEL•	Ialissos	C	96940
MYRTO ••	Ialissos	C	93400
NATALIE•	Ialissos	C	96691/96672
PALMASOL ••	Ialissos	C	93566
ROMA•	Ialissos	C	96447
SUMMER TIME ••	Ialissos	C	23301/90100
SUNDAY ••	Ialissos	C	91921
TASIMARI ••	Ialissos	C	94380
TERINIKOS ••	Ialissos	C	92174
TRIANTA ••	Ialissos	C	94525
VELLOIS•	Ialissos	C	96615
VERGINA ••	Ialissos	C	94386
VILLA REA ••	Ialissos	C	91522
BARBIE ••	Ialissos	C	94490/95280
SUN OF RODOS•	Ialissos	C	—
CASA MANOS•	Ialissos	D	94355
HIPPOCAMPUS•	Ialissos	D	90206
TAKIS ••	Ialissos	D	92543
VIVIAN ••	Ialissos	D	93515
PEFKA•	Ialissos	D	93388/31387
ARMONIA ••	Kremasti	A	29420/93077
KREMASTI VILLAGE ••	Kremasti	A	92424
SUNLAND KREMASTI•	Kremasti	B	91133
SUN FLOWER•	Kremasti	B	93893/94273
ANSELI•	Kremasti	C	94393/92013/91930
ESMERALDA ••	Kremasti	C	94447/92775
GENESSIS ••	Kremasti	C	92798
KLADAKIS ••	Kremasti	C	94208
LIOS ••	Kremasti	C	94346/92134
MARGARITA ••	Kremasti	C	94254
MARITIME ••	Kremasti	C	92232
MATSOUKARIS ••	Kremasti	C	91277
VALENTINO ••	Kremasti	C	91487
MATSIS•	Kremasti	E	91291
ANSELI••	Kremasti		92013
BLUE BAY••	Kremasti		92352/92284
Βόλας Νικόλαος••	Kremasti		91440
G & T.••	Kremasti		91108
ALEX BEACH•••••.	Theologos	A	41634/41612
DORETTA BEACH•	Theologos	A	41440-1
HAPPY DAYS•	Theologos	B	41632/41803
NIRVANA BEACH•	Theologos	B	41127
SABINA•	Theologos	B	41613/41160
SUMMER DREAM ••	Theologos	B	41340/41768
IFIGENIA••	Theologos	C	20310
IVORY ••	Theologos	C	41410/41679

MELITON•	Theologos	C	41666
ASTERIA•	Theologos	D	41712/41602
STEVENSON•	Theologos	E	41557
VALLIAN VILLAGE••••••	Paradissi	B	93727
MARAVELIA ••	Paradissi	C	81210
RHODIAN SUN•	Paradissi	C	81945
SAVELEN•	Paradissi	C	82783
VILLA HELENA ••	Paradissi	C	91175/91243/36827
VOURAS•	Kalavarda	D	41570
THOMAS•	Monolithos	D	61291
NYMPHI•••	Salakos	B	22206
SILIA SORONIS•	Soroni	C	41025
MIRA MONTE•	Maritsa	E	47244
HARAKI BAY•••	Malona	A	51305
GARDEN•	Pastida	C	47008/47900-2
ANAGROS•	Archangelos	C	22248
ANTHI SUN•	Archangelos	C	22619
CARAVOS ••	Archangelos	C	22961
HAMBURG•	Archangelos	C	22978
KARYATIDES•	Archangelos	C	22965
KATERINA•	Archangelos	C	22169
MAIANDROS•	Archangelos	C	22896
NARKISSOS•	Archangelos	C	22436
ROMANTIC•	Archangelos	C	22749/22185
ROSE MARIE•	Archangelos	C	22263
SEMINA ••	Archangelos	C	22210
TSAMBIKA SUN•	Archangelos	C	22568
ARCHANGELOS•	Archangelos	D	22230
FILIA•	Archangelos	D	22604
PHOEBUS•	Archangelos	D	22600
LIPPIA HOTEL GOLF RESORT•	Afandou	A	52007
OASIS HOLIDAYS•••••.	Afandou	A	51771-5
AFANDOU BEACH••••••.	Afandou	B	51586
AFANDOU SKY•	Afandou	B	52347
GOLF VIEW•	Afandou	B	51935
IRIS•	Afandou	B	51664/53300
RENI SKY•	Afandou	B	51125
SIVILLA•	Afandou	B	52326
STAR VIEW•	Afandou	B	52100
CRYSTAL•	Afandou	C	31687
FILIPPOS•	Afandou	C	51933
GOLDEN DAYS•	Afandou	C	52302/52346
ROSE OF RODOS•	Afandou	C	22704
GOLFER'S RESORT ••	Afandou	C	27306
SCALA ••	Afandou	C	51788
KASTELLI•	Afandou	D	51961
NICOLIS•	Afandou	D	51830
ST. NICOLAS•	Afandou	D	51171/52203
SEMIS•	Afandou	E	51525
YIANNIS•	Afandou	E	51565

GOLDEN ODYSSEY•••••.	Kolimbia	A	56401
IRENE PALACE•	Kolimbia	A	51614/56263-7
KOLYMBIA BEACH•	Kolimbia	A	56225
LUTANIA BEACH•	Kolimbia	A	56295
LYDIA MARIS•	Kolimbia	A	56294
MARY ANNA PALACE•	Kolimbia	A	56466
MYRINA BEACH•	Kolimbia	A	56254
NIRIIDES BEACH•	Kolimbia	A	56461/56449/56210
ALFA•	Kolimbia	B	56411
ALLEGRO•••••.	Kolimbia	B	56286
AMERIKANA INTERNATIONAL•	Kolimbia	B	56451
DOUNAVIS•	Kolimbia	B	56212
KOALA•	Kolimbia	B	56296
KOLYMBIA BAY•	Kolimbia	B	56268
KOLYMBIA SKY•	Kolimbia	B	56271-4
LOUTANIS•	Kolimbia	B	56312
MARATHON•	Kolimbia	B	56380
MEMPHIS BEACH•	Kolimbia	B	56288
MYSTRAL•	Kolimbia	B	56346
RELAX•	Kolimbia	B	56220
TINA FLORA•	Kolimbia	B	56251
TROPICAL•	Kolimbia	B	56279
KOLYMBIA STAR•	Kolimbia	B	56437/56419
DELFINIA RESORT•	Kolimbia	B	56601-3
KOLYMBIA SUN•	Kolimbia	C	56213
FANTASY•	Kolimbia	C	56485
EFKALYPTOS	Kolimbia	E	56218
RODOS MARIS•••••.	Asklipio	A	47017/47102/47000
RODOS PRINCESS•	Asklipio	A	43102
HOLIDAY SUN•	Asklipio	B	44133
KABANARIS BAY•	Asklipio	C	43279
KIOTARI BEACH ••	Asklipio	C	43521
VILLA SYLVANA No 1 & 2•	Asklipio	C	23997
PYLONA•	Pilona	D	42207/42447
LINDOS BAY•	Vliha	A	31501-2
LINDOS MARE•	Vliha	A	31130
STEPS OF LINDOS•	Vliha	A	31062-6
STAR OF LINDOS BAY•	Vliha	B	31522-3
STEPS OF LINDOS No 2••••••	Vliha	B	42262
VLICHA SANDY BEACH•	Vliha		31042
YIOTA•	Vliha	B	42205
AMPHITHEATER•	Lindos	B	31351
LINDOS AVRA ••	Lindos	C	31376
LINDOS SUN•	Lindos	C	31453
LINDOS PINES•	Pefki	B	48259
PEFKOS BEACH••••••	Pefki	C	48231/48008-10
SUMMER MEMORIES ••	Pefki	C	41500
THALIA•	Pefki	C	44108
FILIMON•	Pefki	C	48158/44118-9
AMBELIA BEACH•	Genadi	B	44384
BETTY ••	Genadi	C	43020
CHRISTIANA ••	Genadi	C	43228
DOLPHIN ••	Genadi	C	41084
EVANGELOS•	Genadi	C	43082

GENNADI SUN ••	Genadi	C	43057/43453
GENNADI SUN BEACH ••	Genadi	C	43194/43297
GOLDEN SUNRISE	Genadi	C	43003
KAMINDOS ••	Genadi	C	43100/43150
MARITA ••	Genadi	C	43048
OLYMPOS ••	Genadi	C	43256/43029
PANORAMA GENNADI•	Genadi	C	43315
SUMMER BREEZE•	Genadi	C	43314
TINA'S•	Genadi	C	43306/43204
GENNADI BAY•	Genadi	C	43297/43311
SUNSHINE•	Lothiarika	B	44128
KAMARI BEACH•	Lardos	A	44144/44244
ST. JOHN•	Lardos	B	44219/44169
LYDIAN VILLAGE••••••	Lardos		47360-5
NENETOS•	Lardos	B	44209
BEL MARE•	Lardos	B	44252/44248
ILYSSIO•	Lardos	C	48364/48148/48139
LARDOS SUN BEACH••••••.	Lardos	C	44203
LOSTAS•	Lardos	C	44141
SMARA ••	Lardos	C	44264
FEDRA•	Lardos	D	44213
ST. GEORGE LARDOS••••••••	Lardos	D	44249
PARADISE VILLAGE•	Koskinou	A	67040
LE CHEF •••	Koskinou	C	62304
EDEN ROCK•••••	Reni Koskinou	A	67067
PARADISE•	Reni Koskinou	A	66060
SUNWING•••••.	Reni Koskinou	A	66140/62912
CASTELLO•	Reni Koskinou	B	64856
KALLITHEA SUN•	Reni Koskinou	B	62703/62492
VIRGINIA•	Reni Koskinou	B	62041
KALLITHEA•	Reni Koskinou	C	62498
KALLITHEA SKY•	Reni Koskinou	C	62703
LEMONIS •••	Reni Koskinou	C	65958
KRESTEN PALACE•	Kavourakia	A	62714/64612/797
LOMENIZ BLUE•	Kavourakia	B	63344/62480
ATPIUM PALACE•	Kalathos	AA	31601-3/31622-5
KALLIGA •••	Kalathos	C	21961/31150-1
DANIEL•	Kalathos	C	31101
KALATHOS SUN•	Kalathos	D	31661
XENI•	Kalathos	D	31171/31505
AMALIA•	Apolakia	C	61365
SCOUTAS•	Apolakia	E	61251/61282
ΛΑΧΑΝΙΑ•	Lahania	D	43089

- •   Hotel
- ••   Rooms to rent
- •••   Guest House
- ••••   Furnished apartments
- •••••   Hotel & Bungalows
- ••••••   Bungalows
- •••••••   Campsite

(The above numbers have been taken from the National Tourist Organisation's list of hotels for 1994.)

Index of Proper Names

NTO & Tourist Police	F3	Town Hall	F2	Library	F4	General Bank	E2
Telecommunications (OTE.)	E3	Bishop's Redisence	F3	Temple of Venus	F4	National Bank	E3
Post Office	F3	Grand Masters' Palace	E4	Inn of Auvergne	F4	Commercial Bank	E7
Government's Office	F2	National theatre	E2	Temple of Pythian Apollo	B6	Ionian & Popular Bank	E3
Olympic Airways	E3	Aquarium	E1	Ancient Stadium	C5	Real Estate Bank	E3
Austrian Airlines	E3	Evangelismos Church	F3	Ancient Theatre	C5	Crete's Bank	E3
British Airways	E3	Sound and Light	F4	Murat Reis Mosque	F2	Piraeos Bank	E7
Imperia	D2	Archaeoligal Museum	F4	Yacht club	F2	Bank of Greece	F4
KLM	E3	Byzantine Museum	F4	Agrotiki Bank	E3	Pisteos Bank	H6
Cyprus Airways	E3	Folclore Art Collection	F4	Barclays Bank	E2	Costums Control	H4

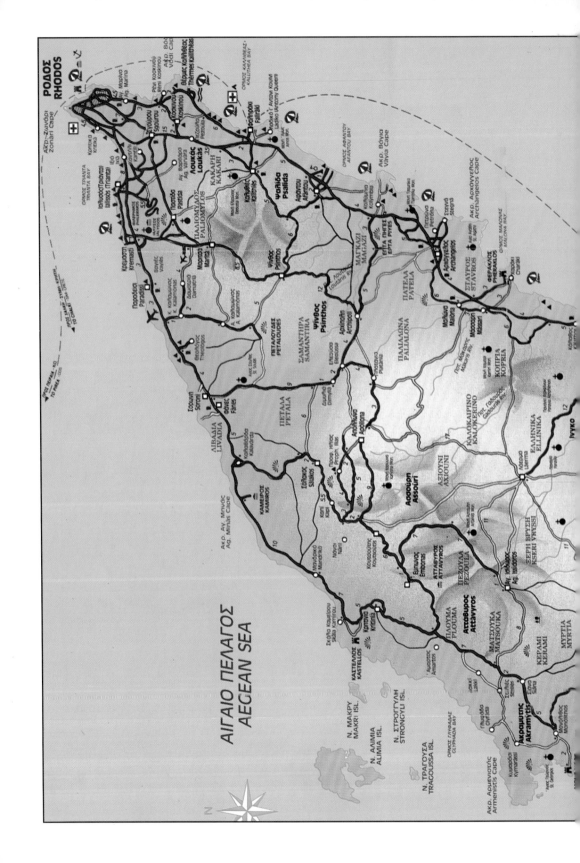